T0311335

'This is an impressive and fascinating introduction to Herbert Rosenfeld's contribution to psychoanalysis, covering all the salient aspects of his thought. His profound capacity for identification with psychotic suffering, observation, and interpretation, along with his ability to encapsulate inner experiences into words, made him a major psychoanalytical figure and allowed us access to a series of insights on the deepest levels of human suffering. Hinshelwood's thoughtful understanding and great accuracy and clarity of writing make Rosenfeld accessible to a wide range of readers. This book not only shows how substantial Rosenfeld's contribution to psychoanalytic thinking and clinical practice was, but also how useful his clinical approach still can be for exploring and understanding psychotic conditions. In my view, this book is the best overview of Rosenfeld's thinking available and I heartily recommend it to any experienced psychotherapist and psychoanalyst, as well as to any advanced student in the field.'

Alberto Stefana, *PhD, University of Pavia*

'Bob Hinshelwood's new book is a compelling introduction into the life and work of Herbert Rosenfeld, one of the most original and creative analytic thinkers in the Kleinian tradition. The author accompanies the reader on Rosenfeld's audacious journey to the most primitive and deepest layers of the human mind, his exploration of psychosis, narcissism and Borderline states, the discovery of projective identification and splitting mechanisms as well as his examination of pathological organizations of the personality. Like the author's previous books it is written with passion and didactic clarity including concise clinical vignettes to illustrate the theoretical issues. The book provides also important information about Rosenfeld's life, his debates with contemporary analysts and his understanding of countertransference entanglements. I think, it is a 'must' for everyone who is interested in the development of psychoanalytic theory and technique.'

Prof. Heinz Weiss, *head of the Department of Psychosomatic Medicine, Robert-Bosch-Clinic, Stuttgart; Member of the Directory Board of the Sigmund-Freud-Institute, Frankfurt am Main; Chair of the Education Section of the International Journal of Psychoanalysis.*

Herbert Rosenfeld

This bold and insightful book is the first to present the full work of highly influential British analyst, Herbert Rosenfeld.

This Contemporary Introduction covers all of Rosenfeld's significant publications between 1947 and 1987, as well as the later edited version of his clinical seminars in Italy. Hinshelwood deftly shows how Rosenfeld adopted Melanie Klein's theories on schizoid mechanisms and psychotic psychodynamics and applied them to working with patients experiencing psychosis. He traces the use of these ideas in an evolving understanding of psychotic states and other forms of disturbance.

This book will be of interest to psychoanalysts and psychotherapists working with the development of Kleinian ideas. It will also be the perfect guide for students, mental health workers and psychotherapists who wish to know more about Rosenfeld's approach to psychotic states.

Robert Hinshelwood is an English psychiatrist and academic. He is Professor Emeritus at the University of Essex, UK. In 1984, he founded the *British Journal of Psychotherapy* and edited it for ten years, and founded the journal *Psychoanalysis and History* in 1999. He is the author of *A Dictionary of Kleinian Thought* (1989).

Routledge Introductions to Contemporary Psychoanalysis
Aner Govrin, Ph.D.
Series Editor
Tair Caspi, Ph.D.
Executive Editor
Yael Peri Herzovich
Assistant Editor

"Routledge Introductions to Contemporary Psychoanalysis" is one of the prominent psychoanalytic publishing ventures of our day. It will comprise dozens of books that will serve as concise introductions dedicated to influential concepts, theories, leading figures, and techniques in psychoanalysis covering every important aspect of psychoanalysis.

The length of each book is fixed at 40,000 words.

The series' books are designed to be easily accessible to provide informative answers in various areas of psychoanalytic thought. Each book will provide updated ideas on topics relevant to contemporary psychoanalysis – from the unconscious and dreams, projective identification and eating disorders, through neuropsychoanalysis, colonialism, and spiritual-sensitive psychoanalysis. Books will also be dedicated to prominent figures in the field, such as Melanie Klein, Jaque Lacan, Sandor Ferenczi, Otto Kernberg and Michael Eigen.

Not serving solely as an introduction for beginners, the purpose of the series is to offer compendiums of information on particular topics within different psychoanalytic schools. We ask authors to review a topic but also address the readers with their own personal views and contribution to the specific chosen field. Books will make intricate ideas comprehensible without compromising their complexity.

We aim to make contemporary psychoanalysis more accessible to both clinicians and the general educated public.

Aner Govrin – Editor

Neuropsychoanalysis: A Contemporary Introduction
Georg Northoff

Herbert Rosenfeld: A Contemporary Introduction
Robert Hinshelwood

W.R. Bion's Theories of Mind: A Contemporary Introduction
Annie Reiner

Psychoanalysis and Colonialism: A Contemporary Introduction
Sally Swartz

Psychoanalytic Field Theory: A Contemporary Introduction
Giuseppe Civitarese

Eating Disorders: A Contemporary Introduction
Tom Wooldridge

Michael Eigen: A Contemporary Introduction
Loray Daws

Christopher Bollas: A Contemporary Introduction
Steve Jaron

Sándor Ferenczi: A Contemporary Introduction
Alberto Fergusson and Miguel Gutierrez-Pelaez

Transgender Identities: A Contemporary Introduction
Alessandra Lemma

Projective Identification: A Contemporary Introduction
Robert Waska

Donald Meltzer: A Contemporary Introduction
Meg Harris Williams

Herbert Rosenfeld

A Contemporary Introduction

Robert Hinshelwood

Routledge
Taylor & Francis Group

LONDON AND NEW YORK

© Michal Heiman, Asylum 1855-2020, The Sleeper (video, psychoanalytic sofa and Plate 34), exhibition view, Herzliya Museum of Contemporary Art, 2017

First published 2023
by Routledge
4 Park Square, Milton Park, Abingdon, Oxon OX14 4RN

and by Routledge
605 Third Avenue, New York, NY 10158

Routledge is an imprint of the Taylor & Francis Group, an informa business

© 2023 Robert Hinshelwood

British Library Cataloguing-in-Publication Data
A catalogue record for this book is available from the British Library

Library of Congress Cataloging-in-Publication Data
Names: Hinshelwood, R. D., author.
Title: Herbert Rosenfeld : a contemporary introduction / Robert Hinshelwood.
Description: Abingdon, Oxon ; New York, NY : Routledge, 2023. | Series: Routledge introductions to contemporary psychoanalysis | Includes bibliographical references and index.
Identifiers: LCCN 2022037799 (print) | LCCN 2022037800 (ebook) | ISBN 9781032380384 (paperback) | ISBN 9781032389424 (hardback) | ISBN 9781003347590 (ebook)
Subjects: LCSH: Rosenfeld, Herbert A. | Psychoanalysis. | Psychoses.
Classification: LCC RC438.6.R67 H56 2023 (print) | LCC RC438.6.R67 (ebook) | DDC 150.19/5092 [B]—dc23/eng/20220816
LC record available at https://lccn.loc.gov/2022037799
LC ebook record available at https://lccn.loc.gov/2022037800

ISBN: 9781032389424 (hbk)
ISBN: 9781032380384 (pbk)
ISBN: 9781003347590 (ebk)

DOI: 10.4324/9781003347590

Typeset in Times New Roman
by codeMantra

Contents

Introduction

An outline for the reader

> This introduction gives a few biographical details and
> highlights the essential elements of Rosenfeld's contribu-
> tion to contemporary psychoanalysis.

This book is for the reader, ordinarily informed of general psychoanalytic ideas. However, the subject of this book, Herbert Rosenfeld, lived and worked in a very specific context, intellectual,
professional and cultural. For readers who want something of this
context, an attempt has been made to detail terms in the Glossary at
the end. Otherwise, as far as I have been able, the text has been written to put the working ideas and practice into ordinary language,
and to illustrate in terms of our experience as human persons.

Rosenfeld was not a particularly original thinker, but an extremely careful and enlightening clinical observer:

> Rosenfeld's particular theoretical approach is a combination
> of his clinical experience with his capacity for – or, one should
> say, art of – observation and interpretation. He had the gift
> of an astounding capacity for identification with psychotic
> suffering.
>
> (Steiner 2001, p. xi)

He is a practising psychoanalyst's psychoanalyst.

His importance is the insights he leads us into that reveal
the deepest levels of human suffering. These are the confusion,

DOI: 10.4324/9781003347590-1

anxiety and conflict of states that in some people emerge as psychotic, and in many others as relentless disturbances of their personalities and relationships. Rosenfeld remains a pre-eminent authority on observing this level of agonised experiencing, and encapsulating it in words and concepts.

A brief biography

Herbert Rosenfeld is hardly a contemporary now, having died nearly 40 years ago. However, there are many people who have been taught by him, who are still practicing today and who are influencing the contemporary world of psychoanalysis. His quiet presence still exists.

He was born in 1910 in Nuremberg – it had been the year of the first international meeting of psychoanalysts, and indeed they met in Nuremberg. He was therefore a second (or perhaps even third) generation of psychoanalysts. He had an older sister and two younger sisters, and his father owned a substantial agricultural business, growing hops.

He did not go into the family business but instead studied medicine qualifying in 1934. In 1936, he came to Britain because as a Jew he was now forbidden to practice as a doctor in Germany. He re-qualified at the medical school in Glasgow. However, as an immigrant he was again not able to practice, and so instead he began training as a psychotherapist at the Tavistock Clinic, qualifying in 1940 and subsequently working for periods at the Warneford Hospital, Oxford, and at the Maudsley Hospital in London. As a refugee from Germany, he was not required for military service even as a doctor. During that time, he began analysis with Melanie Klein and qualified as a psychoanalyst at the London Institute of Psychoanalysis in 1945.

Although, Rosenfeld's parents followed him to England, his three sisters dispersed around the world. In 1941, he married Lottie, another German refugee in the UK, and they had three children, with now numerous grandchildren. Rosenfeld seems to have been a family man, though also very involved in his analytic work which he did in his private consulting room at his home in St John's Wood, in London. It seems that the mysterious work was a considerable fascination for his young children (Angela Rosenfeld

2016). His circle of friends seems to have been largely from the psychoanalytic world.

He was a quiet and serious man with a gentle smile, and clearly, from his writing, showed an open sensitivity to others' experience. It is the latter, his sensitivity to the extreme experiences of others, which made him a formidable psychoanalytic virtuoso. His gentleness appears to have been expressed by his being one of the very first Jewish psychoanalysts prepared to offer supervisions to psychoanalysts back in Germany from, I believe, the 1970s.

Rosenfeld died suddenly in 1986, suffering a deeply debilitating stroke just prior to an evening seminar he was about to hold, and the stroke soon led to his death in hospital. Although aged 76, he clearly still had more to develop in his thinking. His interest and concern demonstrated in his last book made it pointedly sad that it had to be published posthumously. His legacy was not just his professional work, but a generation of analysts for whom he was analyst, supervisor or teacher. My own interest was particularly prompted by that last book, *Impasse and Interpretation* which I read on its publication in 1987, the year after he died. It reviewed in various ways the impact the patient had on the analyst, and the resulting impact on the patient of how the analyst managed that impact.

The analyst's own foibles have an impact on the transference, the analytic progress and the obstructions to the progress. Such a recognition of the possibly major impact of the analyst's own intra-psychic world was not unique to Rosenfeld, but he expressed it most clearly, and sensitively. It seemed enlightening that an impasse could evolve from the intra-psychic worlds of both struggling together.

Outline of this book

I will attempt to illustrate with Rosenfeld's own examples the detailed observations of the main conceptualisations he emphasised, and will capture the main themes of Rosenfeld's thinking over 40 years from his first paper in 1947 to his posthumous books. His work does not easily fall into phases because much of his thinking remained consistent over the years, simply developing slowly. Many of his working tools, drawn from Melanie Klein, remained fundamental throughout his work, demonstrating his continuing loyalty. He asserted a constant claim that his 'technique' remained close to the classical method of Freud's and Klein's. His progress was a deepening of the ideas, a more and more detailed way of using the ideas, and the application of those ideas to more situations, situations which he liked to label with medical diagnostic terms.

It is possible to specify general aspects of his work:

i Perhaps the clearest point that Rosenfeld made all through his work was his conception of confusional states, a confusion over the motivating emotions of love and hate (not distinguished clearly from Freud's 'libido; and 'death instinct').

ii Confusion was so often dealt with by projective (and introjective) processes so that parts of the self were confused with external objects and re-introjected causing a further confusion, a confusion of identity.

iii A core element of the vagaries of aggression was the turning back of the aggression against the self, a negative 'narcissism'; it compares with but contrasts with, Freud's description of libidinal narcissism where the person turns to love themselves as much as, or more than, the world of objects.

iv Despite relying on the classical method focused on the giving of an interpreted meaning, there are actual differences not always exposed by Rosenfeld:

a He sought to work with meanings in the form of a narrative with objects, rather than a carefully measured coaxing of the derivatives of instincts and their energy out of the unconscious, and then the pre-conscious.

b Interpretations were as directly but sensitively given, allowing for the pitfalls of the transference which may distort the act of interpretation (arousing confusion for instance, or envy), rather than allowing a final moment of discovery outside of the conflicts of the transference.

v His aim seems to have been a straightforward use of Melanie Klein's ideas for the adventurous understanding of the more difficult clinical problems, starting with the intractable problem of psychosis itself. This entailed two strategies:

a First, to identify separate categories, usually in diagnostic terms

b Second, to identify core psychodynamic processes or unconscious phantasy (in terms of Kleinian schizoid mechanisms) for each of these different categories

These interests do not comprise distinct phases in the development of his thought. However, they do occur roughly in sequence,
but very roughly. The point is that there is a great deal of overlap
in his publications as he moves from one diagnostic interest to
another and back again. Thus, my individual chapters move back-
wards and forwards in time. The progression tends to be mainly
in the different conditions he identified – from psychosis and
confusional states to narcissism and to borderline personalities,
and to various categories such as addiction or hypochondriasis.
His clinical practice did remain remarkably constant, with an al-
legiance to the technical approach developed by Melanie Klein
(Klein 2017).

However, it is worth noting one trend in his last ten years which
set debate amongst colleagues and subsequent readers of his
work. This was a troubled concern with the way the analyst's own
modes of coping could obstruct (perhaps over long periods) the
full recognition of the patient's suffering.

He was increasingly well-known throughout the 1960s and
1970s and increased his teaching with seminars, especially inter-
nationally. Thus, he became increasingly aware of the pressure
that work with severely disturbed patients put on their analysts. As early as 1953, Melanie Klein had warned of work with
schizophrenia:

> … the patient's violent processes of splitting the analyst and
> pushing into him parts of his self and of his impulses – a pro-
> cess which I have named projective identification – has a most
> strenuous effect on the analyst (Klein 1953, quoted in Hin-
> shelwood 2008, p. 101).

Rosenfeld appeared to become increasingly aware of this strenuous effect, and concerned to help those who attended his seminars to struggle with this especial emotional load (Rosenfeld
1987, 2001). In addition, the developing general interest in

countertransference after the 1950s contributed to that awareness of the interaction, for the good or for the bad, between the intra-psychic unconscious aspects of both the analyst and analysand.

Rosenfeld as a Kleinian

Klein's concepts arising from children's play led to a true para-digm shift in Thomas Kuhn's sense. Klein witnessed the playing out of significant, and anxious relations with toys. Inevitably, her conceptualisations were in terms of the narratives that the toys represented of relations with significant people and anxieties. It is known today as the object-relations school. It by-passed instinc-tual energy and the economic model. For Freud, conflicts and the Oedipus complex, were dealt with by repression and the develop-ment of a zone of unconscious wishes (known as the id). Conflicts therefore remained, but outside consciousness. Then accretions of stimuli/instincts (or drives) were discharged in dreams, in Freud-ian slips, symptoms and long-term personality traits.

However, with her new observations, Klein found processes that disrupted the very coherence and functioning of the mind, rather than conflicts within it. Eventually, over 20 years she found the loss of coherence or disintegration of the self (ego) resulted from the splitting apart or splitting off of mental functions (known as ego-functions). And this was primarily from the splitting apart of love and hate, so that the mental functions create disorganised and separated feelings. Klein held that her model was quite com-patible with Freud's, but merely operated at a different depth, and she repeatedly talked of the 'deeper layers' of the unconscious. The integrity of the self (or, 'ego') has obviously to be established before conflicts *within* the ego can be dealt with. So, in the classi-cal model, energy (felt as anxiety) provokes repression out of con-sciousness. But in the object-relations model, the anxious conflict of feelings provokes much more basic problems of integration.

Rosenfeld inherited Klein's model when he turned to psychotic symptoms and diagnoses. Though Klein risked pathologizing that deeper layer of disintegration and self-destructive splitting by calling it psychotic, she intended a contrast with the Freudian layer of more straightforward neurotic mental conflicts. In fact, the processes she was assigning to the deeper layers, were quite normal for the very young infant, but remained evident in psychotic states because of an excessive and persisting use. A true psychosis can only be recognised as a later excessive and dominant use in adult life of what appears familiar in the earliest infant's experience. This early and deeper layer, known as the paranoid-schizoid position, was explored by Klein and her colleagues in the early development and then in later pathology. Rosenfeld was at the beginning of these investigations with her. He was treating an adult patient, Mildred, from 1944, who exhibited many of these mental processes, and his observations provided supportive evidence for the new model Klein was about to propose in 1946.

Summary of the ideas

The key ideas that emerged in Rosenfeld's clinical work were:

- Unchanged classical technique
- Schizophrenia and homosexuality
- Confusional states (hate and love)
- A persecuting super-ego precursor
- Negative narcissism
- Psychotic transference
- Entangled countertransference

The chapters follow this skeleton of ideas.

Note: a preliminary warning on 'phantasy'

This note is more than introductory. It is a clarification for the whole book about the model of the unconscious mind which Herbert Rosenfeld adopted. At the level of the unconscious, there is a constant slippage in our awareness between what is the material world of reality and what are our own perceptions in our minds. We can often see what we imagine to be real, but our real world is not exactly as we might expect on the basis of these templates we keep in our mind. Such templates are known technically as our "unconscious phantasies".

This is a philosophical position – we see shadows on the wall, as Plato graphically described it, and elaborated by the German philosopher, Immanual Kant. Psychoanalysis grew up within this tradition where the human mind contributes as much to our own perceptions as does the real external world; and the sensations from the interior of our bodies are coloured by the templates of unconscious phantasies. So, for instance when we see the colour red – at the traffic lights, perhaps – our eyes, the sense organs, do not receive the colour. They receive an electromagnetic wavelength, between say 600 and 700 nanometres. The mind, correlated with our brain's activity, changes the material reality into a mental experience – in this case, the colour red. Similarly, with physical objects; the solidity of the desk I am working at is only about 1% matter, and the rest is a space occupied only by forces. We can also wonder about time itself – does it exist only in our minds? The philosophical answer is unknown. But, for our minds, time does exist. We live our lives according to narratives that stretch out in time, creating a sense of causality. Such narratives prove extremely tempting for humans and we constantly place causality where mere correlations or even chance events occur.

We can however check our run-away narratives by constantly trying to somehow know the reality out there. As Freud (1911b) formulated, we have methods of checking the real material world. The reality principle comes to dominate the human mind. However, such narrative phantasies remain as a bedrock anticipation, composed of innate expectation, such as the breast to suckle as well as the most powerful early experiences. Psychoanalysis asks us to understand this unconscious level of anticipation, which occurs in parallel as our development achieves a dominance of the reality principle.

Especially with psychotic states, we will encounter a dominance of those inner constructions. And to a degree, our experience is put together for us from both sources to create stories that make sense to us. What our minds perceive is always filtered through a demand to compose narratives of meaning and causes. Even for the sanest of us, we can make 'common-sense' that includes some elements of phantastical meaning-making arising from the unconscious background of our minds.

Hence, when we use the term "phantasy" we mean that unconscious level of narrative experience. 'Fantasy' we restrict to conscious imagining such as day-dreams. For some further clarification, see "Unconscious phantasy" in the Glossary.

Part I

Research into difficult problems

Rosenfeld pioneered the use of Klein's observations of schizoid mechanisms, and researched the serious disturbances. It led to various conceptualisations which were progressively refined.

With an initial experience in psychiatry, Rosenfeld tended to use medical types of diagnosis to identify distinct problems he investigated. First and foremost was the challenging difficulty that Freud and others found with schizophrenia. He was the first of the famous 'troika' that included Hanna Segal and Wilfred Bion, and his was their first Kleinian account of the psychoanalysis of adult schizophrenia (considered in Chapter 1). Klein (1930) had reported a case of a very disturbed child, Dick. He would now be regarded as severely autistic, but this had been an important moment that prompted Klein to observe the psychodynamics of the schizoid mechanisms.

Starting with his diagnostic approach, Rosenfeld applied Klein's psychodynamic descriptions, producing papers between 1947 and 1965, and later. He also turned to other diagnostic categories. For instance, his early paper in 1949, developed a psychodynamic view of the connection between schizophrenia and homosexuality strikingly at variance with Freud's (1911a) understanding of the Schreber case.

Thereafter from the mid-1960s. Rosenfeld's style of thinking showed a noticeable evolution influenced perhaps originally by his analysis with Melanie Klein (see Steiner 2008). He moved somewhat from grasping the patient's experience, however difficult in psychotic states, to develop a stronger emphasis on

DOI: 10.4324/9781003347590-2

metapsychological terminology and classification in the latter papers in his book *Psychotic States* (1965). He turned to the phases of libidinal development, the model of fixation and regression and so on. This fitted with his systematic diagnostic style as he surveyed and investigated other difficult categories beyond psychosis (see Chapter 7). Then, in his last decade based perhaps on his seminar work, he moved back again towards experiential descriptions of the experiences of the analyst and patient entangled in each other's unconscious psychodynamics (see Part 2).

Fundamental from the beginning, and at the root of all the conditions he explored, were confusional states. He revealed the basic and often muddled interaction from the beginning of life between hate and love. This presents the new-born with the disturbing need to unravel the two mental states from each other (Chapter 2). Almost as fundamental were the mechanisms for doing so, splitting of the ego (and of objects) and projective identification (Chapter 3). Whatever the reality, the complex mechanisms lead to a clear separation of hatred, often ending up as a cruel, critical and punitive internal object he regarded as a harsh forerunner of the super-ego (Chapter 4). At times that painful development itself goes wrong, and the hateful and destructive part of the *ego* turns upon itself, creating an internal battleground of self-destructiveness (Chapter 5). That re-arrangement of the self has become a crucially important formulation of the more stable borderline personalities, to the present day.

Chapter 1

Mildred and features of psychotic states

This chapter demonstrates some of Rosenfeld's very first observations at the outset of his training. These observations with Mildred formed a basis for the conceptual developments that lasted throughout his life and have greatly influenced the recent generations of psychoanalysts.

Mildred was a training case when Rosenfeld was a candidate. He was allowed to embark on her treatment even though she suffered psychotic states (published 1947). In March 1944, when she started, Mildred was 29 years old. She had a poor relationship with her father, – was the oldest of three children with a brother only 19 months younger. After his birth she was separated for some weeks from her mother. As a child she attempted to imitate her brother, seemingly because of his popularity with everyone.

In her twenties, Mildred was able to join up for volunteer work during the wartime. However, she was not able to sustain it, but subsequently worked as an assistant in a bookshop. She did not report auditory hallucinations nor compelling delusions, but several features suggested psychosis at the time Mildred was sent for analysis by her parents. These were characteristics of psychiatric disorder, though sometimes called second-order symptoms: First, a blankness of affect, and this impacted on the analyst as an impenetrable lack of relationship; a resulting tendency to be silent especially when a degree of intimacy was referred to in interpretations; then a sense of herself as in pieces or in some way not

DOI: 10.4324/9781003347590-3

fully herself; and finally a problem in keeping a continuity in her thinking (for instance, she knew how long it would take her to get somewhere but could not use that knowledge to give herself the time she needed to arrive).

Clinical features

There are a number of features in Mildred's mental state that Rosenfeld emphasised and which illustrated Klein's schizoid mechanisms; these are:

- Periods of blankness and silence
- Her problem of feeling 'joined up'
- Others became concrete representations of parts of herself
- Identifications
- Confusional states

Periods of blankness and silence

Rosenfeld noted her problem with feelings:

> At times when describing her experience she would say that there was something like a blanket separating her from the world, that she felt dead, or not here, or cut off from herself. At other times she called these feelings "deadlock feelings".
>
> (Rosenfeld 1947, p. 132)

Moreover, she felt no shock or reaction on the death of her brother when he was killed in an accident. This schizoid blankness differs from repression when a blankness of mind is not characteristic, instead, with repression, there is a speedy substitution of a replacement idea.

Rosenfeld also described:

> [When] there seemed a small improvement in her condition, but the slightest difficulty, particularly any positive transference interpretation, produced long-lasting silences, and when she was able to speak again she related that she had experienced some of the schizoid symptoms I enumerated just now.

As usual there was an amnesia of everything we had discussed previously.

(p. 132)

This repeated blankness, especially connected with her positive feelings is typical of splitting.

Her problem of feeling 'joined up'

And more specifically she said: "if she tried to join up with herself, she might force her mind completely out of joint" (p. 132). This is a very conscious expression of an experience of joining up, or not. But most of us when under tension feel we cannot get our thoughts together or our words don't make sentences. We can sometimes talk about 'going to pieces'. Or, we also talk of people who seem crazy, that they 'have a screw loose'. This sense of coming apart is not unknown as an experience of quite ordinary people. However, Mildred was much more disabled. It became absolutely fundamental from the beginning of Rosenfeld's writing, indeed from the beginning of his working practice.

Others as representations of parts of the self

A really significant observation was the strange almost out-of-body experience that Mildred conveyed. She used others to attribute parts of herself to: "[H]er object-relations at this stage were very insecure, and on analysis it turned out that more often than not the other people represented a part of herself" (p. 132). And:

Apart from the projection of impulses which were felt by the patient to be bad, there was a continuous projection of good impulses also into other people, particularly women friends, who not only represented good mother-figures, but the good part of herself. She felt excessively dependent on these friends and could hardly function without them.

(p. 132)

This is a description of how significant parts of her 'self' were felt as part of the identity of others – because those close and dependent attachments were felt as parts of herself. There is here an instability and 'fragility' of her own ego. It is similar to the experience in a group, perhaps an emotional group, a fan club for instance when everyone cheers and idolises some incomparable celebrity. That infectious 'togetherness' has some affinity with the phenomenon of projecting something of oneself into another person so that there is a profound feeling in common. But in the case of the more primitive process, it becomes a confusion about who one really is.

Identifications

The sense of some part of herself going into another person created a complex ambiguity about Mildred's identity: "when she met people she might one day find herself talking in a strange voice or accent. This voice would have talked, I am certain, with the analyst's voice and accent" (p. 134). This identification with the object (the other person) is reflected again in another patient:

> The patient had the greatest difficulty in differentiating himself from the analyst. For example, he had a dream where a German professor on a motor bicycle tried to split himself in two by running against a gate-post. In this dream the splitting mechanism was increased by the fact that the patient felt himself so confused with the analyst.
>
> (Rosenfeld 1949, p. 44)

It was as if he could only feel separate from the object he had projected into, he needed a great force or violence to separate.

Confusional states

For Rosenfeld, confusion became a fundamental experience at the beginning of life. He was already familiar with the idea that love and hate are primary emotions from the beginning. How can an infant see the difference? He/she has no real experience, and no real basis for labelling things one way or another. Hence

Rosenfeld thought there is likely to be a constant risk of confusion from the first moments:

> I suggest that under certain external and internal conditions when aggressive impulses temporarily predominate, states may arise in which love and hate impulses and good and bad objects cannot be kept apart and are thus felt to be mixed up or confused.
>
> (Rosenfeld 1950, 32–33)

A patient in a psychotic confusion

Trying to sort out good from bad was illustrated by Rosenfeld in one of his earlier very disturbed patients. He described the first session:

> [H]e sat down in a chair looking very puzzled and confused. After a few minutes he managed to say one word, 'RESURRECTION'. After that he again looked confused.
>
> (Rosenfeld 1952b, p. 459)

There is definitely an odd quality to this opening. The single word 'resurrection' does not invite a coherent conversation. There is a serious difficulty in connecting with the analyst. But Rosenfeld, with some experience now of the meanings behind these odd expressions, had a hunch:

> I said, "Resurrection means to become alive". He looked straight at me and said, "Are you Jesus?"
>
> (p. 459)

At that moment, Rosenfeld noticed a fleeting change; the patient looked straight at him. So, he followed the theme, trying to give a more coherent meaning to these opening remarks:

> I said that Jesus could do miracles and that he hoped I would make him well in a miraculous way. He then looked distressed and uncertain, and after a considerable silence he mentioned

the name of Dr. A. who had treated him by physical methods for over a year.

(p. 459)

The idea of miracles distressed the patient, perhaps because of memories of Dr A's failed treatment. But despite that, the patient responded – obscurely again:

After another long pause, he said, 'Catholicism'. I interpreted that he had believed in Dr. A. and he felt disappointed because the treatment had failed.

(p. 459)

If the patient was in fact distressed as Rosenfeld had noticed, it is quite possible the patient would be doubtful at the first session of a new treatment, and would be uncertain about what to expect:

He then replied with emphasis, "The Russians *were* our allies". I replied that he felt that Dr. A. had been an ally and had now turned against him, and he was afraid that I also would turn from an ally into an enemy. He then said clearly, "This is true'.

(p. 459)

Understanding his uncertainty about whether he could expect something good did seem to touch the patient. It led the patient to formulate a meaningful sentence relevant to Rosenfeld's interpretation. And that more coherent connection between them continued:

He became now more rational and talkative and mentioned a number of his sexual problems, for example, circumcision, which he thought was a form of revenge, and he said, "I do not understand love and hate".

(p. 459)

The development from incoherence to more meaningful communications was of significance. It shows that after all some meaning can be found in psychotic utterances. In other words, the analyst's attempt to find meaning connects in such a way that the patient can indeed find coherence in himself again. This experience of being understood has, one can assume, had some beneficial impact on the disconnections. Some sort of clarity could occur about what is good and what is bad. Not only are the Russians good or bad, but is the analyst good or bad? It is no longer a confusion. This meaningful sequence, starting with Dr. A as hope, had continued into disappointment.

However, it is not so simple. Later in this more hopeful initial session between them the patient said, still coherently:

> "There was a boy at school"; after a pause he continued, "He sat beside me, the trouble was – a boy was sitting on the other side of him".
>
> (p. 459)

Though apparently still coherent, what was its meaning? Rosenfeld again intuited an understanding, basing it on the patient's appreciation of what had been achieved, however slight:

> I interpreted that he began to like me as he liked the boy at school; but he wanted me to himself, and he realized I had other friends and patients.
>
> (pp. 459–460)

Once the patient felt understood, Rosenfeld became a good analyst for him – but then a negative. The patient came back to a reality – sharing and then jealousy. There is a penalty if he understood the meaning of reality. The painful jealousy and exclusion sent the patient back into his distress. He had agreed to the meaning that Rosenfeld's last comment verbalised, but it had placed the patient in a dilemma again – how to handle a good experience with ensuing pain:

> [S]oon after this he became restless and got up from his chair and said, "One must get out at once – I better go now", and later he mumbled, "I must have a saw." I thought he was afraid of his jealousy of other patients and that he wanted to get away to prevent himself from hating and attacking me.
>
> (p. 460)

This last point of Rosenfeld's which he verbalised to the patient did not remove the distress:

> After pointing this out to him, he still remained restless until the end of the hour.
>
> (p. 460)

But the understanding did, perhaps, enable the patient to stay in the room. One could say perhaps it enabled the patient to stay with the restless distress. It was however an achievement. He gained coherence and meaning, instead of the confusion of good/bad in his psychotic state.

Envy in the background

The idea of a confusional state was an idea which I think was given further strength when in the mid-1950s there was considerable contention in the British Psychoanalytical Society over the nature of envy. Envy, in common language, is conveyed by the saying "biting the hand that feeds you". It is both a biting hatred, and a highly needed dependency for survival. For the infant, the two alternative emotional states are difficult to separate, and in addition cause considerable anxiety, even to an infant. Rosenfeld said:

> These infantile states of confusion are states of disintegration and are related to the confusional schizophrenic states of the adult.... The confusional state is associated with extreme anxiety, because when libidinal and destructive impulses become confused, the destructive impulses seem to threaten to destroy the libidinal impulses.
>
> (Rosenfeld 1950, 32–33)

This is different from the confusion of self with another person, but Rosenfeld thought they were related. The confused mixed feelings become a confusion of identity when coherence is attempted by projecting one set of emotions into another person:

> [I]f normal differentiation between good and bad objects and libidinal and aggressive impulses cannot be achieved, splitting mechanisms become reinforced. For example, as a result of the confusion between the good and bad breasts, the phantasy of the good breast may be projected outside and the phantasied bad persecuting breast, identified with bad fæces, may be kept entirely within the patient.
>
> (Rosenfeld 1960, p. 134)

Thus an attempt to sort out the confusion between the feelings can be achieved by separating in terms of two identities. However, the risk then becomes a confusion between the two identities.

So, a number of different things can be discovered in this desperate separation – notably separating good from bad parts of the self, but also separating good and bad objects. Three kinds of separation can be in play:

- Confusion is most disturbed where there is some recognition of difference but it cannot be properly tracked down;
- Then there is the splitting where the different parts of the self or objects which are kept as far apart as possible and definitely out of contact or communication; and
- The third is the least disturbed which is a normal form of ordinary conflict where different opinions, needs or impulses come together as ambivalence, needing resolution. It is not comfortable, but love and hate remain coherent, and if sustained becomes a developmentally mature state; it allows the testing of objects and of one's own feelings against the reality of the world out there (and indeed inside the self).

The importance of confusional states will be returned to in Chapter 3.

The primitive state and the psychotic state

From 1947, Rosenfeld specified the anxieties that provoke extreme defence measures which fragment the ego and its capacity to know

one's identity or where one is. He summarised it in a later paper
(Rosenfeld 1969). Reviewing historically the psychoanalytic views
on psychosis, he noted:

> Freud was aware that excessive strength of instincts played an
> important part in psychotic states but did not discuss specific
> psychotic conflicts between parts of the self, such as loving
> and destructive parts of self, based on his theory of the life
> and death instincts. He regarded the main conflict in psycho-
> sis as a conflict between the ego and reality.
>
> (Rosenfeld 1969, p. 617)

Following Freud, much of the work that has been done on psychotic states has used the rejection of reality as its starting point.
Freud (1911a) described how Schreber, the mad lawyer, rejected
his perception of external reality and substituted his own views.
He constructed a world of delusions and hallucinations which he
then lived within. For Freud, the reality was Schreber's physician
who aroused unacceptable homosexual desires. Schreber disman-
tled the whole of his perception of reality in the process of repudi-
ating and repressing his homosexual impulses. It gave Freud the
opportunity to understand how a person in more normal development acquires their sense of the real world. The 'reality principle'
comprises six ego-functions and Freud (1911b) described them in
the same year he wrote about Schreber. With a loss of interest in
reality, the ego redirects the whole of its attention to the self. And
in particular, as with Schreber, the ego fascinates itself with its
own imagined world.

A few years later Freud (1914) described narcissism – it is primary, i.e. arising at birth. It is from that state of being oblivious
to the world around that the ego has to extricate itself by the development of its perception and the 'reality principle'. But where
reality is repudiated, an unreality remains as a psychotic state.
And so, Freud called the psychoses the "narcissistic neuroses".
But Rosenfeld, following Klein, disagreed. There was no primary
state of narcissism which the self/ego has to work its way out of.
Klein's observation and analysis of very young children indicated
the opposite and suggested that the withdrawal into psychosis

pointed to an anxiety that precedes narcissism and concerns the feelings of good versus the bad. So, narcissism is *secondary* to that conflict and confusion. And developing a narcissistic focus on one's unconscious phantasy aims to avoid those states in the very young infant, and in psychosis.

Chapter 2

Projective identification and depersonalisation

> One of the most persistent features of his early case, was Mildred's use of other people who could become disowned aspects of herself. The merging or confusion of personal identity with others was significant for her. Whilst splitting was the important fundamental 'mechanism', or unconscious phantasy, it is closely connected with another phantasy, the fate of the split-off bits. These can be disposed of by evacuating them into others, the phantasy (or mechanism) labelled 'projective identification'. In effect it removes part of a person from themselves.

Rosenfeld described in the title of his first paper how Mildred suffered from a 'depersonalisation'. This was a word that Klein did not use but it represents the effect of the mechanism of projective identification which Rosenfeld began to emphasise from the outset and continued to the end of his life. The term 'depersonalisation' covers the sort of out-of-body experience that Mildred had described as not joined up.

Klein had been considering the deeper layers of the unconscious since 1934 (Hinshelwood 2006). However, for various reasons, it took her until 1946 to formally publish the seminal paper, 'Notes on some schizoid mechanisms'. Klein thought that the mechanisms dealing with anxiety in the very early stages of infant development were comparable to those mechanisms still manifest in adult psychotic states although distorted and excessive as she put it.

DOI: 10.4324/9781003347590-4

However, by the time she published her paper, Rosenfeld had already completed his paper originally for qualification as a Member of the Psychoanalytical Society and presented privately to members of the Society. He described the work with Mildred which depended on just the mechanisms that would go into Klein's paper. Her paper had covered the model of 'splitting' of the ego in a more general sense while he described a case study in detail.

Melanie Klein gave an initial description of projective identification:

> [B]ad parts of the self are not only meant to injure but also to control and take possession of the object. In so far as the mother comes to contain the bad parts of the self, she is not felt to be a separate individual but is felt to be the bad self.
>
> (Klein 1946, p. 8)

This is illustrated in Rosenfeld's account of Mildred (Chapter 1). Aspects and parts of her 'self' really were believed to be in the other person.

This appears a strange kind of occurrence. However, we could consider as an example the ordinary blame game between two people – for example, two drivers who bump their cars. Both accuse the other in an aggressive argument. There is a symmetry, like a tennis match, in which each throws accusations at the other. Carelessness, inadequate driving, guilt and shame are projected violently into each other. Each feels themselves to be the accused 'bad' driver' and then projects it all back again, gaining a righteousness. Such an incident demonstrates how some integral part of the self – the 'guilty' driver – can be repudiated (split off) and seen convincingly as the other driver. It resembles the kind of vendetta between the Montagues and Capulets who engaged (in Shakespeare's *Romeo and Juliet*) in a special relationship with each other; they did not leave each other alone. Each needs the other to be the bad one. The tennis match is relief and retaliation performed by projective identification.

Although this may be a familiar sort of experience, it does have complexities. In particular, the attribution of a part of the self to another, weakens the self, and at the same time creates a degree of confusion about where one is located.

Another further complexity is the projection of a *good* part of the self into the other person. Then, the other person becomes identified with the self in its good aspects. That idealisation of the good other also contributes to a penetrating kind of intimacy, but it also provokes a seriously lowered value of oneself and a weakening dependency.

These observations of Klein's have their precursors in Freud's writing. First the projection of the bad, Freud wrote:

> Expressed in the language of the oldest – the oral – instinctual impulses, the judgement is: "I should like to eat this", or "I should like to spit it out"; and, put more generally: "I should like to take this into myself and to keep that out." That is to say: "It shall be inside me" or "it shall be outside me". As I have shown elsewhere, the original pleasure-ego wants to introject into itself everything that is good and to eject from itself everything that is bad. What is bad, what is alien to the ego and what is external are, to begin with, identical.
>
> (Freud 1925, pp. 236–237)

This set of processes amounts to narcissism, to which Rosenfeld will contribute shortly (Chapter 5).

Freud also described the opposite, an idealisation when a good part of the self is attributed to another person:

> The impulsions whose trend is towards directly sexual satisfaction may now be pushed into the background entirely, as regularly happens, for instance, with a young man's sentimental passion; the ego becomes more and more unassuming and modest, and the object more and more sublime and precious, until at last it [the loved other] gets possession of the entire self-love of the ego, whose self-sacrifice thus follows as a natural consequence. The object has, so to speak, consumed the ego.
>
> (Freud 1921, p. 113)

These descriptions were followed up by Klein's (1946) and Rosenfeld's (1971b) authoritative accounts. I now propose to consider Rosenfeld's account of projective identification in some detail.

Psychotic transference

The International Psychoanalytic Association held its Congress in London in 1953; it held sessions devoted to the analysis of schizophrenic conditions, one on the psychology of schizophrenia and one on the therapy of schizophrenia. Rosenfeld's paper (published 1954) headed the second of these (and the first was the occasion when his colleague, Bion, gave his first presentation on psychosis).

One of the main points, Rosenfeld described is that the kind of transference developed in such disturbed patients is a psychotic one. His idea of a psychotic transference meant a relationship with the analyst where the patient uses the analyst to split himself and objects, the analyst *becoming* those parts. The analyst no longer *represents* some other figure as in a neurotic transference. The analyst *becomes* the split off parts. Typically, a 'neurotic' transference means the analyst represents an Oedipal figure. In contrast, in a psychotic transference the analyst enables a splitting and projection of parts of the self, ego-functions and intolerable experiences by becoming them.

So often these transferences are enacted in non-verbal ways. That is to say, instead of communicating a representation the patient makes a direct impact on the analyst, on his feelings, on his self. It is not conveyed in symbolic communications of dreams or words, or replaced as significant others elsewhere.

Rosenfeld presented the case of Anne who clearly experienced herself getting inside someone (or equally, someone else getting inside her). When she started analysis, Anne was so anxious she had to have her mother with her in the consulting room. She often made efforts to get out of the room:

> I noticed that she was looking at the ceiling in a confused and frightened manner. I interpreted that she felt shut in somewhere, but she was not sure whether she was inside me or in somebody else.
>
> (Rosenfeld 1954, p. 137)

Rosenfeld made a hunch that Anne's gazing at the ceiling expressed her anxiety of being shut in a dangerous place which necessitated keeping mother with her to protect her.

When I said this she looked much more frightened at first, but her attempts to escape from my consulting-room lessened. I repeated my interpretations in slightly different ways. After some time she did not look quite so confused and made some attempts to speak.

(p. 137)

Again, the understanding Rosenfeld gained from his observations of her bodily expression enabled a gradual relaxation in Anne, and eventually she could speak:

She then asked me whether my room was the same and later she said she was very mixed up and she did not know how she got into my room. She became more confiding, and said: "I want to tell you something. I was walking along in the park and I was quite cool. Suddenly I had a blackout and then I was in somebody else's coat". I pointed out to her that she had suddenly gone into somebody else and consequently felt mixed up with somebody else. I also explained in some detail that she was experiencing the same situation with me.

(p. 137)

The verbal material conveyed an enclosed experience similar to the one that Rosenfeld had described. She called it a blackout, quite a severe experience. Was Anne, merely following Rosenfeld's lead in looking at things in this way? Patients can often oblige the analyst by taking up what they think the analyst is interested in. This may have been the case but in fact with Anne it was more. Ann actually was the analyst:

She then looked at me for quite a time and said: "Why do you imitate me?" I interpreted that she had put herself into me and that she felt that I was her and had to talk and think for her. I explained to her that this was the reason why she felt so shut in when she came to my house and why she had to escape from me. She was now looking much more comfortable and trusting, and said: "You are the world's best person".

I interpreted that because she felt I was so good she wanted to
be inside me and have my goodness.

(Rosenfeld 1954, p. 137)

There is a considerable change during the course of these interventions. Rosenfeld's understanding her location of her 'self' actually
inside the analyst, was a turning point. It enabled the patient to
feel less terrified. The point here is that Anne experienced a change
of who she is by changing where she located herself – now in him:

This interview illustrates some dynamics of the acute schizophrenic process and the way it is influenced by interpretations. Following the interpretations that the patient felt she
was inside me, she was able to extricate herself out of me
which lessened her confusion. She then became more aware
of me as an external object and was able to talk.

(p. 137)

The confusion about the mix-up of selves could be sorted out as
Anne experienced her anxiety being understood by another person. The emphasis here is on the mobile relocation of the self. It
is not just splitting the ego but the projective identification of the
self.

From the work with this patient, Rosenfeld could conclude:

In the acute schizophrenic state the patient tends to put his
self so completely into objects that there is very little of the
self left outside the object. This interferes with most ego-
functions, including speaking and understanding words. It
inhibits the capacity to experience relations with external objects and it also disturbs the introjective processes.

(p. 138)

By 'introjective processes' Rosenfeld was indicating how Anne listened and could take something into her own mind, into her own
self. In one sense, that internalisation process makes us the children
of our parents. We take on their ideas and behaviours and as we

grow up we assess and chose what we will take as a part of our own selves, and to become part of who we are. This is a normal process, and it contrasts with the kind of process Rosenfeld was describing where there is a failure of this experience of taking on the features of the parents, and instead there is a confusion with *being* the parent. It is a set of two contrasting experiences which is difficult perhaps for most of us to envisage. However, many of us will occasionally be confronted by someone (a wife or husband, typically) saying, "Oh you are just like your mother" (or father, etc), and with surprise we had never really thought that out. It is a surprise and then a stimulus to reflect on that observation we have been given.

Rosenfeld noted how this process converged with some of the observations made by other analysts (Jacobson 1954, Mahler 1952) where the ego merged with other identities, or a symbiosis. Others conceptualised the fusion/confusion as a primary state of the ego, Freud's primary narcissism. It is a sort of total unseparated absorption from the beginning of life. Rosenfeld presented Klein's view as a contrast; it is a secondary and defensive narcissism.

'Projective identification' is one of the most important of the technical terms Rosenfeld used. He assumed the earliest infant had a sense of self and of a separate other, even though the boundary might be subsequently penetrated with a loss of separateness and a confusion of identity. The loss of identity results from projective identification as a penetrative intrusion that avoids feeling a catastrophic loss of love and a confusion with the triumph of hate.

Whether projective identification is a protective measure of that kind, or narcissism is a primary experience out of which the infant has to emerge and grow, is a critical difference between schools. We cannot hold to both – that a person is both merged with others at birth, and at the same time has a boundary to the self.

Forms of projective identification

Rosenfeld eventually described several radically different forms of projective identification. One, he attributed to Bion (1959), a communicative form. It is not the radical evacuation of a part of one's self, and not in the interests of a narcissistic repudiation of what is bad in the self. Instead, it is a *communication* with another person. The object is required not to be merely a receptacle for what is bad. The intention is to communicate with another who is assumed to have a mind that can therefore experience the badness for the infant (or analysand).

The aim is a co-ordinated projection on the part of the patient and an introjection on the part of the analyst:

> He then projects impulses and parts of himself into the analyst who will feel and understand his experiences... so that they lose their frightening or unbearable quality.
>
> (Rosenfeld 1971b, p. 121)

It is thus a very direct transfer of feelings. The transfer is not mediated by words. However: "[They] become meaningful by the analyst being able to put them into words through interpretation" (Rosenfeld 1971b, p. 121). And the patient in some more receptive part of his mind recognises the symbolic meanings of the analyst's words and can absorb (or introject) the analyst's meaning-making functioning. He gradually takes it as his own functioning and accumulates a degree of meaning-making.

It is important to differentiate this communicative intent from the evacuative projective identification. Crucially, the patient can receive back a communication about the constructive efforts of the analyst. But in the evacuative form, the patient is likely to feel interpretation is a retaliatory attempt at violent re-evacuation into the patient.

Rosenfeld distinguished a third form of projective identification – neither an evacuation of bad shaming parts of the self, nor the non-symbolic communicative form. He described:

> As a third point I want to discuss a very common transference relationship of the psychotic patient which is aimed at controlling the analyst's body and mind.
>
> (Rosenfeld 1971b, pp. 122–123)

This controlling intention is difficult for the analyst who may feel he cannot therefore offer anything the patient does not have. The patient feels self-sufficient. In Rosenfeld's terms the patient is in a state of 'omnipotent' narcissism; that is to say the patient feels he now possesses everything he needs to do for himself:

> As long as the patient regards the analyst's mind and body and his help and understanding as a part of his own self he is able to attribute everything that is experienced as valuable in the analysis as being a part of his own self, in other words he lives in a state of omnipotent narcissism. As soon as a patient begins to feel separate from the analyst the aggressive reaction appears and particularly clearly so after a valuable interpretation, which shows the analyst's understanding.
>
> (Rosenfeld 1971b, p. 123)

Until he possesses the analyst, the patient feels humiliated and small. He thinks: "why should the analyst remind him of something which he needs but cannot provide for himself" (Rosenfeld 1971b, p. 124). This state of hating the one who provides was emphasised by Melanie Klein as envy (Klein 1957) – "biting the hand that feeds you". So, Rosenfeld made the categorical comment:

> I believe that in the psychotic patient projective identification is more often a defence against excessive envy which is bound up with the patient's narcissism, rather than a defence against separation anxiety.
>
> (Rosenfeld 1971b, p. 125)

The defence against envy is to control and take possession of the analyst's talents and to identify with them; that identity is a narcissistic solution to the envy. Separation then is not just the loss of a narcissism, but it opens up the humiliation of needing and dependency, and implies lesser gifts or self-worth.

A case briefly

The dynamics of projective identification are desperate and Rosenfeld illustrated the painful problems resulting in depersonalisation. With a diagnosed schizophrenic patient (referred to as

Patient A), Rosenfeld had to interrupt for two weeks. At first
the patient took the information in his stride, but as the time approached he became more and more disturbed:

> The disturbance started with the patient's complaint that he
> could not drag himself away from the television screen where
> he was watching the Olympic games. He felt forced almost
> against his will to look at it until late at night.
>
> (Rosenfeld 1971b, pp. 129–130)

There was a compulsive quality to watching the television as if
stuck to it perhaps:

> He was also compelled to look at the athletes, or wrestlers
> and weightlifters and felt he was, or ought to be, one of them.
> He asked me questions: "Why have I to be an athlete? Why
> can't I be myself?"
>
> (Rosenfeld 1971b, p. 130)

Quite consciously he was struggling with an identity issue which
made him feel unable to be himself:

> At times he felt so strongly "pulled inside the television" that
> he felt claustrophobic and had difficulty in breathing... I in-
> terpreted to him that after he felt that he was making progress
> and feeling separate from me he was suddenly overcome with
> impatience and envy of me and other men who were able to
> move about and were active.
>
> (Rosenfeld 1971b, p. 130)

The approaching break indicated the analyst was a man with the
freedom to be himself and to move about, a person represented by
the athletes going to Mexico:

> I suggested that it was the envious part which drove him into
> the identification with other men and myself in order to take

over their strength and potency, and in this way the omnipotent part of himself could make him believe he could be mature and healthy instantly.

(p. 130)

He agreed with all this and expressed his anger with himself for being persuaded of these delusions. The disturbing event – the disruption to his regular sessions and the independence of his analyst – threw Patient A into a very different and disturbed form of relationship with objects and others. In this case, there was another side of the patient, It was a side to which Rosenfeld could talk, and could listen and understand his own reactions to the disturbance.

The benign forms of projective identification

These various uses of projective identification result in the loss of the sense of being a person to some degree (depersonalisation). But Rosenfeld considered various beneficial and less violent forms:

> One can even think of psychoanalysis as a specific instance in which free associations can be thought of as projective identificatory externalization which allows the patient to grow through externalizing his inner mental content for interpretation, leading to self-assessment (Grotstein, 1982). I also believe that some projective identification is involved in the process of object cathexis, a term which is still used by some analysts. There is also the projection and externalization of aspects of the self in order to recognize objects and to identify with them, or to look for objects for the purpose of making essential links with them. These are all processes of projection and externalization necessary for developing object relations.
>
> (Rosenfeld 1983, p. 264)

He included these forms as benign communicative projective identification. In all cases, there is a need for careful scrutiny:

> In all projective or externalizing experiences in analysis the consequence of the projection has to be carefully scrutinized by the analyst as it is difficult for the patient to assess his own emotional experience and particularly his behaviour. He generally cannot himself observe what is going on in some sessions, or sometimes even in the whole analysis while these projective processes are being acted out.
>
> (Rosenfeld 1983, p. 264)

The analyst has the task of assessing the form and purpose of such intimacy of projection and identity. In a normal development, the next step is to bring together these split apart bits of self and object. They need placing in relation to each other, as a conflict and not as a split bits. In later childhood and adulthood, the Oedipal conflicts of incestuous love and patricidal hate must come together, though agonising. One might put it like this: if both parts of the self which are split apart, or which are confused, can be put clearly into a *single* interpretation without confusion then there is a possibility that the person can take into themselves that understanding as two sides of a conflict instead, thus offering the beginnings of an integration again.

Rosenfeld was aware of Bion's discussion of the complexities of communication in this way, and when it fails. Bion recognised failure as 'attacks on linking', on the communicative linking. Communication is not itself immune from envy and attack, and thus of a swift conversion to a form of control and possession, and then of retaliatory persecution.

Chapter 3

Confusional states

Rosenfeld's earliest work described the fundamental states of hating and loving and how difficult they are to distinguish from each other. Much of Rosenfeld's work from the beginning was to establish the various dynamics of these earliest confusions. This chapter brings out the various aspects of Rosenfeld's observations on the early confusion and its later manifestations.

At the Zurich IPA Congress in 1949, Rosenfeld set out his considered view on confusional states. He found them to be fundamental in most disturbed states of mind. His basic point, that love and hate are confused at the very beginning, prompts the infant to deal with it in equally primitive ways, often with disturbing consequences.

Over the course of the next few years, he gave observations, descriptions and some theorisation of these states. In summary there were the following characteristics:

- First and foremost is the use of projection of one or other state into others to accentuate a discrimination between love and hate
- Second is a specific form of reparation which is badly interfered with by the hate, leading to incoherent reconstruction of self or other
- Third, by successfully locating hate in another person that other becomes a violently retaliatory object

DOI: 10.4324/9781003347590-5

- Then fourth, is that at the beginning there may be a convergence (or confusion again) between projection and introjection so that the other hate-filled object is felt as internal and becomes the self-destructive super-ego
- However fifth, the realisation of these processes in the transference enables the analyst to interpret as they happen with the visible result that the patient may 're-take' himself

I propose to describe each of these five formulations in more detail with some illustration from Rosenfeld's own descriptions.

Splitting self and other

When confusion is avoided through splitting, it leads to paranoia and idealisation. Nevertheless, it is an advance on confusion and aims at a defence against confusion. In this case, the early developmental problem of getting love and hate distinct, is intimately connected with the psychotic problem of getting one's identity clearly:

> I wish to draw attention to my observation that the schizophrenic patient whom I am discussing here and all the schizophrenics I have investigated show one particular form of object-relationship very clearly; namely, as soon as the schizophrenic approaches *any* object in love or hate he seems to become confused with this object.
>
> (Rosenfeld 1954, p. 458)

The primary inevitably involves the object towards whom emotions are felt. The resulting splitting and projective identification lead inevitably to entering the object including the analyst. Two results occur:

- First, a lost sense of self with a withdrawal from connection and impaired mental functioning including the concrete kind of communication
- And a second confusion of identity – confused with primary objects, and with the analyst

Repairing hindered by destructiveness

Libidinal impulses emerge as phantasies of repairing the ego as well as repairing objects who in his phantasy he has damaged or destroyed completely. Rosenfeld described a highly disturbed and inadequate form of reparation:

> However, when aggressive impulses become temporarily pre-dominant, the reparative process may be interfered with in a particular way. The libidinal impulses succeed in bringing the pieces of the objects and the ego together, nevertheless the aggressive impulses prevent the pieces from being sorted out and put together correctly. In the worst instance, the objects and the ego become pieced together but in a completely mixed up and faulty way. The result is a state of confusion.
>
> (Rosenfeld 1950, p. 137)

In his early papers, Rosenfeld gave many examples of the incoherence of patients verbal communication, illustrated in the previous two chapters.

Confusing projection and introjection

Another aspect of the confusion is that entering the object gets confused with taking the object into himself: "only at a later stage of treatment was it possible to distinguish between the mechanisms of introjection of objects and projective identification, which so frequently go on simultaneously" (Rosenfeld 1952b, p. 463). That is, a patient (see illustration below) projected into father or the analyst, but also in drinking in he was taking his objects into himself.

The retaliatory object

Hate and destructiveness separated off into another person, makes them into a retaliatory and violent enemy, and this may then be re-introjected as a destructive super-ego, or at least a precursor of the super-ego. And to this we will turn in the next chapter.

In the transference

Rosenfeld noted:

> One important transference aspect which was dealt with in this session was the tendency to leave parts of the self in the analyst. This is important for the analyst to understand, because the interpretations of the processes of projective identification and splitting enable the patient gradually – to use my patient's words – "to retake himself", which is necessary for the process of ego-integration.
>
> (Rosenfeld 1952b, p. 462)

Here Rosenfeld is describing the immediate transference process in the session.

We return to the patient already introduced in Chapter 1 to illustrate these various struggles in sorting out the confusion.

An illustration

The very disturbed man in Chapter 1 illustrated these points; he had been brought by his father from another country. The father had just left again before this session:

> In the beginning of the session the patient looked a little confused but, without waiting for any comment or help from me, he said clearly, "Confused", and, when I questioned him, he added, "with father". After a struggle for words, he said, "*I should* have stayed longer". I pointed out that he showed how "confused" he felt with his father, because he obviously meant that his *father* should have stayed longer.
>
> (Rosenfeld 1952b, pp. 461–462)

Father's leaving had de-stabilised the necessary distortion of identity. Here confusion is a defence against the reality of his own identity, and the rage at his father for leaving:

> He immediately went on to say, "Dr. A. committed suicide, through psychiatry, I mean". I pointed out to him that he also confused Dr. A. with himself.
>
> (Rosenfeld 1952b, p. 462)

Father' absence was similar to his previous treatment with Dr. A. who had terminated the treatment and passed him on to Rosenfeld:

> When Dr. A. stopped treatment he, the patient, was depressed and suicidal, but he felt he had put his depressed and suicidal self into Dr. A. I related this to his father's departure and I reminded him how often he had shown his fear that I too would leave him. He then said, "Atheism". I said he wanted to tell me he could not believe in anybody any more after his disappointment about his father leaving him now and earlier too in his life.
> (Rosenfeld 1952b, p. 462)

The patient had previously linked his belief in cure with the miraculous cures of Jesus. His mood improved at this point and he became more talkative:

> He said, "If one goes all the way one cannot retake everything". I then interpreted that when he loved somebody and believed in him or her, he wanted to go all the way, which meant to him that he went inside the other person and so he got mixed up and confused. He also felt that when he put himself into people he had difficulty in taking himself out again. I said it was very important to him that I should understand how much he put himself into me, and that this was one of the reasons why he was so afraid to be left, as he feared he would not only lose me but himself.
> (Rosenfeld 1952b, p. 462)

This is a long and complicated interpretation of the meaning in his utterances. But the patient agreed, and said:

> "A big-boned man eats a lot" and he made chewing movements. I said he was warning me of his greed and he showed me that, in his loving wish to get inside me, he was eating me up. He then uttered a great number of words, referring to the country of his birth, and he talked about colours. It was clear here that he felt a need to stress his separateness, and that the different colours represented different aspects of himself, a fact which we had understood before.
> (Rosenfeld 1952b, p. 462)

The idea of separateness was now in his mind, stirring him a good deal. There is an indication here of putting together 'words' and colours as an illustration of how random bits were 'sliced' apart as an attempt at a kind of discrimination (see Chapter 6).

The patient also referred to the colour pink, a 'code-word' for homosexual desires; and he then got up and very concretely demonstrated by taking a jug of water and drinking it withdrawing from contact with the analyst:

> I interpreted that when he was drinking, he had a phantasy of drinking from my penis and chewing it up. I suggested that the wishes to get inside me stimulated his wishes towards my penis. In his withdrawn state he felt confused with me, because he not only felt that he was inside me, but that he was eating me and my penis at the same time. He again became more attentive, he seemed to listen carefully and he agreed several times.
>
> (Rosenfeld 1952b, p. 462)

The interpretation of his confused eating and internalising the analyst brought him back into a more separate and communicative relation to the analyst. As Rosenfeld said it is the concrete oral impulses which dominate: "This led here to a state of confusion… the patient was unable to speak and other ego-functions like coordination of movements were severely disturbed" (p. 462). Chewing up and swallowing were strongly disturbing because of the confluence of destructive and loving appreciative feelings.

At this stage, Rosenfeld was expressing considerable confidence in the way such interpretations to the patient of the confused state can change that state so that the patient becomes significantly more related and coherent, albeit sometimes dejected. Rosenfeld also noted here as in much of his work (and it is true of his colleagues – notably Bion), that the movement of limbs and face is a significant means of expression.

Some theory

But Rosenfeld did not describe in detail the abnormal kind of splitting until he wrote about borderline states (Rosenfeld 1978b;

see Chapter 5). He described then how a more arbitrarily splitting, or 'slicing' as he put it, is substituted for a reality-based differentiation of good feelings from bad and the good objects from bad, as well as the self from objects. In these states, the various bits only randomly differentiated remain unfortunately confused.

In line with Klein (1957), Rosenfeld understood envy – hating the loved one – as the basis of confusion. This central paradigm, however, remained a little uncertain. He debated whether the confusion is a primary state, prior to splitting, or whether envy is provoked by a stimulus – the experience of separation leading to dependence, humiliation and weakness compared with a loved and needed object. The latter is more convincing because it gives a stimulus to negative feelings and thus places them in the same category as libido which also arises from a stimulus. Of course, a major difference is that the stimuli for libido are bodily (the erogenous zones, etc), whereas for envy the stimulus is relational/emotional.

Rosenfeld thought that there continues to be some danger of being thrown back into the state of emotional confusion. Even as an adult we ask of ourselves; "Am I hate-filled or love-filled?", and if undecided it leads to a crisis of who one is in every sense. Rosenfeld did not put it quite in this way and emphasised again that identity becomes a crisis when the problematic emotions and parts of the self are put into others. That is to say, projective identification distorts how the other person is seen; it is *they* who hate (or love). Then splitting, with projective identification, allows some stability of identity, despite the weakening and depletion of the self, and a distortion of the reality of others.

In conclusion

Rosenfeld point to confusional states and the loss of self as underlying many other categories of patients as well psychotic states. He asserted that this failure is due to the provocation when hate out-balances the satisfaction sf love. As we have seen, his understanding of the causes of hate come from two causes; first the actual neglect of an external other, and second, envy and the humiliation of dependent needs which sever the connection with good objects – Rosenfeld made reference to Bion's (1959) 'attacks' on the good links.

Chapter 4

Super-ego

Relocating parts of the self, especially hatred, into others has a malignant quality so that the other person is experienced as violent and aggressive. They are then regarded with fear as if a confirmed enemy. If the resulting persecuting object is then internalised, as so often in psychosis, that hate-filled enemy becomes a very hostile internal criticiser inflicting cruel punishments on the self (or ego). This internal enemy is very typical of psychotic states and becomes a precursor of a self-destructive super-ego.

Analysts of different schools disagree on the origins of the super-ego and whether it exists as part of a personality prone to psychotic states. Persecution and paranoia are such a strong feature of schizophrenia, but are they the attacks of a super-ego? Freud described the super-ego, as the heir to the Oedipus complex and therefore arising as late as the third year of life as a child moves into the latency period. So, if schizophrenia is postulated as a regression to very early stages of development it would be long before the resolution of the Oedipus complex. On the other hand, from observation, it could be claimed that something like a self-critical function does exist very early on. One observation was Klein's (1932) description of her work with little Rita, a child of 2¾ years. Rita's play showed clear evidence of conflict between her ego and a super-ego-like toy, an elephant. The elephant was put on watch at night-time to stop Rita going into her parent's bedroom and harming them. Moreover,

DOI: 10.4324/9781003347590-6

the symptoms that arose from this ego/super-ego conflict began when she was 18 months old.

Rosenfeld, aware of the divergent opinions, postulated a solution: "I shall distinguish between the early and the later superego" (Rosenfeld 1962, p. 258). The early super-ego is persecutory, cruel, punitive and moralising as would be expected in the black-and-white world when love and hate, and good and bad are split as far apart as possible. It is very inhibitory, whilst the later super-ego shows shades of criticism, guilt and punishment, and acquires benign, encouraging and reparative qualities.

Both in the very early mind and in adult psychotic states, other people are split into exclusively good or bad. However, external objects may then be absorbed (or introjected) to become a part of the internal structure, but, he said: "in many chronic and borderline schizophrenic patients both the idealized and the persecutory objects seem to have some super-ego functions" (Rosenfeld 1952a, p. 114).

Clinical observation

Rosenfeld gave an example of a man hospitalised for a psychotic condition. He seemed troubled by his aggression towards women, and thought one way of dealing with it was to be re-born as a woman:

> Sometimes his aggression turned outward and he attacked nurses, but frequently it turned against himself. He then spoke of "Soul being killed", or "Soul committing suicide", or "Soul being dead"; "Soul" being clearly a good part of himself. Once when we discussed these feelings of deadness, he illustrated this turning of his aggression against himself by saying "I want to go on – I don't want to go on – vacuum – Soul is dead", and later astonished me by stating clearly "The problem is – how to prevent disintegration".
>
> (Rosenfeld 1952a, p. 118)

Rosenfeld says he had never used the word 'disintegration' with the patient, implying the patient's truly felt experience, and he took it as aggression turned against the patient's self. He indicated this conflict, whether to go on or not, as if the struggle within himself was to live or not. It was more than just guilt, it was an omnipotent self-condemnation:

> In fact, on one Saturday, he had attacked a nurse when she had tried to give him an affectionate embrace. His unlimited aggression as if omnipotent and irresistible made him feel he had destroyed the whole world. His sense of guilt was as omnipotently destructive. After that assault he became dejected and silent for two sessions the next week. His behaviour, gestures, and the few sentences and words he uttered, showed that he felt he had destroyed the whole world outside, and later on he said, "Afraid". He added, "Eli" (God) several times. When he spoke he looked very dejected and his head drooped on his chest. I interpreted that when he attacked Sister X he felt he had destroyed the whole world and he felt only Eli could put right what he had done. He remained silent.
>
> (Rosenfeld 1952a, p. 118)

This profound reaction of guilt grossly exaggerated his act in an omnipotent way. He had destroyed everything in the world. This coloured his perception of the world he lived in and what he took from it:

> [I]t is very important to realize at this stage that he felt he had taken the destroyed object, the world, into his ego. The guilt and depression were related to the task of restoring this inner world, which acted as a super-ego, but his omnipotence failed him.
>
> (Rosenfeld 1952a, p. 119)

He felt both the guilt inside him and the retaliatory persecution from outside, and so felt an inner destruction. As he said bitterly:

> [H]e stared at the table and said, "It is all broadened out, what are all the men going to feel?" I said that he could no longer stand the guilt and anxiety inside himself and had put his depression, anxiety and feelings, and also himself, into the outer world.
>
> (Rosenfeld 1952a, p. 118–119)

Rosenfeld conveyed the pressure of super-ego guilt, responsibility and punitive demand for retaliation contributed to the destructive splitting of the ego. There is a potential vicious circle here as the guilt presses on the ego, it splits up, is projected and lost leading to a depletion of the ego with a loss of resources for dealing with the pressure of super-ego persecution now enhanced by the increasing projections and so on.

The assault on the nurse was, Rosenfeld conveyed a displacement at the weekend in which the patient's neediness aroused his omnipotent anger towards an external object (the nurse in this case):

> A very predominant anxiety in the analytic situation, which the patient on rare occasions was able to formulate, related to his need for me. My not being with him on Sundays seemed at times unbearable, and once on a Saturday he said, "What shall I do in the meantime, I'd better find someone in the hospital"... On another occasion he said, "I don't know what to do without you." He stated repeatedly that all his problems were related to 'Time', and when he felt he wanted something from me it had to be given 'instantly'.
>
> (Rosenfeld 1952a, p. 118)

In the actual analytic setting the helping analyst was slowly lost and turned into the external figure created by the projection of the rage at needing the analyst. The analyst's efforts were then compromised:

> [H]e was afraid of what I was going to put back into him, which had the result that his introjection processes became severely disturbed. One would therefore expect a severe deterioration in his condition, and in fact his clinical state during the next ten days became very precarious. He began to get more and more suspicious about food, and finally refused to eat and drink anything.
>
> (Rosenfeld 1952a, p. 119)

Rosenfeld continued to interpret this narrative of his externalisation (hitting out) and fear of internalising damage and destruction. Occasionally, he would reply "Yes" or "No". As Rosenfeld explained:

> It seemed to me that the relevant point had been his inability to deal with his guilt and anxiety. After projecting his bad,

damaged self into me, he continuously saw himself every-where outside. At the same time, everything he took inside seemed to him bad, damaged, and poisonous (like fæces), so there was no point in eating anything.

(Rosenfeld 1952a, p. 118)

The taking in of what he needs, both psychically and in the most bodily form became a threat after his destructive event:

[H]e also felt as if he had inside himself all the destroyed and bad objects which he had projected into the outer world: and through coughing, retching, and movements of his mouth and fingers, he indicated that he was preoccupied with this problem.

(Rosenfeld 1952a, p. 119)

The narrative of this process is that his aggression had hit out at something in a manner that seemed to destroy the world. But, that external object then punished him with a reactive guilt which showed no leniency or compassion. The whole world was nothing but a persecuting object that would fill him up with retaliatory damage and destruction. His capacity for interchange with the world and with the analyst shut down.

This kind of super-ego manifestation is not heir to the Oedipus complex with the management of mixed feelings – desire and murder towards primary objects. Thus, it is a forerunner coloured by excessively bad objects. It is a core element of psychotic states and equates with the 'world catastrophe' that Schreber mourned and which Freud (1911a) understood as central to schizophrenia. However, the world destroyed was understood in a different way by Freud, as were the consequences. Freud understood the catastrophe as a total loss of interest in the external world – a de-cathexis. Any desire, interest or attention to what might be of interest had been completely foregone in order to repudiate Schreber's own homosexuality which terrified him.

For Rosenfeld, it was different. He did acknowledge a connection with homosexuality. However, instead of those desires being so disapproved of it led to paranoia, it was the other way around – a tendency for paranoia led to homosexuality (Rosenfeld 1949, and see Chapter 7 in this book).

The consequences are also different. For Freud, the withdrawal of all interest in real others, and an absence of engagement or relationship with the analyst meant no transference. Such narcissistic patients, Freud argued cannot be analysed. But for Rosenfeld, engagement continued. The connection was however the projective identification of elements of the self and the psychotic transference. Parts of the self enter the analyst and deplete the subject who exhibits a blank withdrawal and a silent sort of 'absence' in the analytic session.

Generally, this early super-ego-type of figure emerges from these primitive processes in which objects cross the ego boundary in this manner:

> When there are phantasies of the self entering the mother's body aggressively, to overwhelm and to take complete possession, we have to expect anxiety, not only about the mother and the entering self being destroyed, but also about the mother turning into a persecutor who is expected to force herself back into the ego to take possession in a revengeful way. When this persecutory mother figure is introjected, the most primitive super-ego figure arises which represents a terrible overwhelming danger to the ego from within. It is most likely that the inability of the schizophrenic ego to deal with introjected figures depends on the peculiar nature of this early object relationship.
>
> (Rosenfeld 1952a, p. 120)

It was important for Rosenfeld to capture just how distorted the real others are when perception is so interfered with by the projections. The needed maternal figure (the nurse who embraced him or the analyst needed at the weekend) became instead the receptacle for the projected hatred at the neglect. So, neglect became transformed into maternal rage and retaliation. Rosenfeld concluded that:

> In most transference psychosis in borderline patients the analyst is misperceived as an omnipotent, sadistic superego.
>
> (Rosenfeld 1978, p. 218)

However, many other transferences may alternate with the disabling super-ego persecution:

> I have seen patients who first formed a transference psychosis which was dominated by the sadistic superego and which after some time suddenly switched over into a delusional, erotic transference psychosis. This observation would confirm the peculiar nature of this primitive superego, which has both sadistic and erotic seductive components.
>
> (Rosenfeld 1978, p. 218)

One of the important aspects was not just observing the reactions of the patient aroused by the needs for defence, evacuation, containment, etc. but also by reactions in the analyst. Or, to put it another way, the patient's defensive needs interact with a counter-transference reaction in the analyst as Rosenfeld (1987) described in his later book. In psychosis the transference is the actual relocation, projective identification, into the analyst, although patients less disturbed may skilfully play upon the analyst's reactions for purposes of defence or evacuation deploying a communicative form of projective identification. The subtlety of these combinations is very difficult for the analyst to identify and discriminate. Rosenfeld, as we shall see, later emphasised such intersubjective unconscious collusions.

Because this precursor super-ego presents itself as the outcome of the fundamental conflict between hate and love, some say that Rosenfeld ignored the specific moral quality of super-ego attacks. However, Rosenfeld was of course speaking of a precursor. And even so, it does indeed refer to qualities of 'good' loving and 'bad' hating. Good and bad are seen especially in terms of neediness and neglect which come to have moral values. Those early interactions are particularly virulent and aggressive, and may persist in adult psychotic states. That is, the person and his conscience live in a persistently aggressive and punitive relationship.

Chapter 5

Negative narcissism

Freud had called psychotic states the "narcissistic neuroses". However, Rosenfeld realised he was describing
something different, opposite even. It was not self-love
but about self-hate. His elaborate model of the cruel and
primitive super-ego brought bitter self-destructiveness
into a personality who suffer psychotic states.

First of all, Freud's view of the "narcissistic neuroses" was based
on his reading of Judge Schreber's memoirs. Schreber had been
an eminent German judge who suffered a severe psychotic break-
down, was hospitalised and developed a permanent set of delusions about a grandiose role he played after a catastrophe to the
world which pushed onto him the responsibility for repopulating
civilisation. This paranoid delusion arising from his own imagination became his reality.

Freud thought this state of self-involved interest was the initial
state of mind into which we are born (Freud 1914). Partly from
the Schreber's memoirs, Freud could understand this state in infancy and in psychosis. Such a narcissistic turning away from external reality with an abolition of the real world, was the core of
psychosis.

However, it really only gave rise to the next question; why does
external reality have to be repudiated? The answer is that external reality poses threats and so the self denies and rejects reality.
Psychotic states are, for Freud, a persistence of a primary state re-
gressed back to or never properly relinquished. This differs from

DOI: 10.4324/9781003347590-7

the neuroses that Freud concentrated on, where the person has sat-
isfactorily moved well enough from their primary narcissism, and
have used aspects of the real world to mitigate their own problems.
It also differs from Klein and then Rosenfeld who postulated an
alternative. Life does not start with narcissism and move towards
an increasing acceptance and detailed acknowledgement of reality.
Instead, what Klein observed in the play of very young children
was a harsher confrontation with reality from the beginning typified by the prohibiting super-ego figure. One instance was the case
of Rita (Klein 1932, mentioned in Chapter 4), where her symptoms
originated as early as the age of 18 months.

Turning away from reality to an exclusive attention to the self
is a defensive manoeuvre, for Klein, it is not a regression to an
earlier primary state of pre-genital narcissism close to an infantile
state of mind. Instead, Klein traced the narcissism to a conflict
in the present, and Rosenfeld identified: "the specific psychotic
conflicts between parts of the self, such as loving and destructive parts of self, based on [Freud's] theory of the life and death
instincts" (Rosenfeld 1969, p. 617). That primary psychotic conflict may become one between the ego and the super-ego (as in
Chapter 4). The raw anxiety of hating and loving, dealt with by
splitting becomes the actual separation between two parts of the
ego. So, it is conflicts in internal reality which lead to the narcissistic rejection of external reality.

Now, the critical turn that Rosenfeld made was to see that turning love inward towards a self-love was not the only possible form of
narcissism. He proposed a negative form in which *negative* feelings
are turned towards the self. Loving the satisfactions of a generous
person is as primary as hating a person who frustrates, deprives
or debases. Hence, he could see that the self-destructiveness of
splitting can be seen as a parallel narcissism – destructive towards
the self, instead of nurturing. Turning aggression back on the self
to split the ego is a 'negative narcissism' (Rosenfeld 1972).

Moreover, 'narcissism' is not simply turning away from others
but various relations *with* them:

> Psychotic patients seemed typically to show omnipotent
> attitudes to others and particularly to their therapists.

In phantasy they seem to make insatiable demands on their objects, to confuse self and others, to take others into themselves, and to put themselves into others.

(Rosenfeld 1987, p. 20)

Thus in these psychotic transferences, others become the self in some form or another. These reactions to others and use of them can be self-enhancing, just as the dependence on others can seem very belittling. A more lordly dismissal and denial of the significance of others endows a greater sense of self, the grandiosity of arrogance and omnipotence.

This was Rosenfeld's most significant postulate: *negative feelings can be turned towards the self as well as one's positive loving libido.* Klein's model of splitting and the whole spectrum of schizoid mechanisms could then be encompassed in his understanding of a negative form of narcissism (Rosenfeld 1971).

Personality organisation

This alternative form of narcissism offers an explanation for disturbed psychological states that are not overtly psychotic. But the explanation is in terms of object-relations theory rather than the classical Oedipus complex and instinct theory. Rosenfeld described in his patient Anne (see also Chapter 2), how the Oedipus complex might appear looked at from the point of view of his model.

Whereas Freud would have described Anne's psychotic state as deriving from a genital conflict, involving father and mother, Rosenfeld saw it differently. For instance. at the start of her psychoanalysis, she would not stay in the analyst's room without her mother:

At the beginning of each session Anne seemed to take no notice of me, but it was soon clear that she was trying to use the presence of the mother to re-enact some aspects of the oedipal situation, in particular to accuse her and devalue her in my eyes. She said, for example, that the mother was a murderess, had sold her for £5, and had made her have the disgusting electric shock treatments and injections.

(Rosenfeld 1954, p. 136)

This at first appears like a narcissistic withdrawal; she took no notice of the analyst. However, she did concentrate on her mother in the room. And she expressed her bitter devaluation of her mother. This was to support the inestimable value of Anne herself. She could thereby achieve a grandiose and narcissistic state; omnipotence, self-idealisation and self-sufficiency. However, that state is sustained at the damaging expense of the object, mother or analyst.

But then:

> In one of the next sessions Anne changed her attitude and said her mother was wonderful, there was nobody like her in the world.
>
> (Rosenfeld 1954, p. 136)

This shows the second side of her feelings for her mother. It emerged that there was also a full appreciation – not only the superiority she initially showed. The painful conflict between a singular love and idealisation as well as the bitter hate were split apart – in time. For Rosenfeld the splitting dealt directly with the basic anxiety of loving and also hating, and both feelings existed in an unmitigated form, but could only exist separately. These are Anne's response to a conflict of emotions towards her mother. The anxiety arose from a primary conflict between them. That conflict seemed to continue to be Oedipal and was not a regression from it. Her withdrawn state was not a regression to a primary narcissism.

Rosenfeld claimed evidence of his Kleinian view because the process that followed was significant. After interpreting the confluence of opposite emotions eventually Anne emphatically agreed with him, and Rosenfeld commented: "After this I gave the mother a sign and Anne allowed her to leave the room for the first time" (Rosenfeld 1954, p. 136).

Rosenfeld's interpretation had a powerful effect. He had not interpreted a state of narcissistic withdrawal due to a conflict-evading regression, but instead interpreted that she was in a continuing conflict of emotions towards her mother. That interpretation of her conflict enabled Anne to feel secure enough that she could let her mother leave the room. Rosenfeld was claiming that the constructive effect of the interpretation implied that the enduring intense emotions for the object remained active.

The core conflict was not about the mother herself, but about the patient's impossibly conflicted feelings that destroyed the integrity of her own self. Her management, or rather mismanagement, of these states of conflicted mixed feelings was so difficult that a psychotic state evolved. The term narcissism here means the use of others to manage the state of one's self. It is the characteristic of the "psychotic transference", as opposed to a neurotic transference where other people are displacements and thus *represent* primary figures.

The importance of these primitive mechanisms and of negative narcissism gained more general interest. So, in 1971, Rosenfeld was invited to present his work to the International Psychoanalytic Association Congress in Vienna. The paper, published the same year, is perhaps his best known, and most applied, of all his contributions. The organised splitting of the personality is more complex than the one encountered in psychotic states, and more elaborate than the description of Anne's 'narcissistic' personality above.

Whereas Klein had described a process of disintegration and fragmentation typical of psychosis, Rosenfeld found that in less psychotic people the split in the ego was more organised, in one a loving libidinal self, and in the other destructiveness – the 'negative ego'. Whilst Freud had discussed the fusion and defusion of the two instincts, Rosenfeld described the splitting of the ego:

> Melanie Klein stressed that split-off, unconscious envy often remained unexpressed in analysis, but nevertheless exerted a troublesome and powerful influence in preventing progress in the analysis, which ultimately can only be effective if it achieves integration and deals with the whole of the personality.
>
> (Rosenfeld 1971a, p. 172)

A greater focus on the relations between the two parts of the self is needed in conjunction with objects in the external and internal world.

Clinical illustrations

A patient kept his object relations in a deadened state, by deadening the lively (libidinal) part of himself that could enjoy other's company:

> One narcissistic patient... dreamt of a small boy who was in a comatose condition, dying from some kind of poisoning. He was lying on a bed in the courtyard and was endangered by the hot midday sun which was beginning to shine on him. The patient was standing near to the boy but did nothing to move or protect him. He only felt critical and superior to the doctor treating the child, since it was he who should have seen that the child was moved into the shade.
>
> (Rosenfeld 1971a, p, 174)

This is a dream of a part of himself left to die by the negative ego:

> The patient's previous behaviour and associations made it clear that the dying boy stood for his dependent libidinal self which he kept in a dying condition by preventing it from getting help and nourishment from the analyst.
>
> (Rosenfeld 1971a, p, 174)

Unfortunately, Rosenfeld does not give those previous associations, so it is merely plausible rather than evidence:

> I showed him that even when he came close to realizing the seriousness of his mental state, experienced as a dying condition, he did not lift a finger to help himself or to help the analyst to make a move towards saving him, because he was using the killing of his infantile dependent self to triumph over the analyst and to show him up as a failure. The dream illustrates clearly that the destructive narcissistic state is maintained in power by keeping the libidinal infantile self in a constant dead or dying condition.
>
> (Rosenfeld 1971a, p. 174)

The narrative is that a part of the patient sought help from the analyst. It was a dependent part of the patient and in need of the analyst. So, the patient's libidinal ego which sought life and living could only survive with help and the relationship with a significant object, i.e. the analyst in this moment. But that part comes up against, not an external bad object, but a destructive part of itself that insists on a deadly neglect of this libidinal self:

> Contact with the analyst meant a weakening of the narcissistic omnipotent superiority of the patient and the experience of a conscious feeling of overwhelming envy which was strictly avoided by the detachment.
>
> (Rosenfeld 1971a, p. 174)

This powerful resistance, a negative therapeutic reaction, could lift at times, after an interpretation of the narrative. However, the deadening would usually close in again quickly. Rosenfeld persisted in describing the structure and process in a narrative form:

> [It is as] if one were dealing with a powerful gang dominated by a leader, who controls all the members of the gang to see that they support one another in making the criminal destructive work more effective and powerful.
>
> (Rosenfeld 1971a, p. 174)

There is an interplay between the dominance of the libidinal ego and the dominance of the negative ego. It resembled the dream of another patient about the relations between a mafia gang and the rest of the population. In a psychoanalytic treatment: "the defusion of the instincts has gradually to change to fusion in any successful analysis" (Rosenfeld 1971a, p. 172); in other words, the capacity to integrate has to outshine the negative ego. Rosenfeld drew attention to the idealisation of the omnipotent destructive parts of the self:

> They are directed both against any positive libidinal object relationship and any libidinal part of the self which experiences need for an object and the desire to depend on it. The destructive omnipotent parts of the self often remain disguised or they may be

silent and split off, which obscures their existence and gives the impression that they have no relationship to the external world. In fact, they have a very powerful effect in preventing dependent object relations and in keeping external objects permanently devalued, which accounts for the apparent indifference of the narcissistic individual towards external objects and the world.

(Rosenfeld 1971a, p. 173)

The self-idealisation of one's omnipotent destructiveness is not altogether rare, for instance, spontaneous aggression outside a pub on Saturday evenings, or on the football terraces in 1980–1990s Britain. What Rosenfeld was emphasising was that the emergence of this aggressive object-relationship also involved an internal aggression in which an omnipotent negative ego dominates the libidinal part of the ego.

Rosenfeld was particularly gifted in exposing these narratives, as if especially in touch with the dream world of the patient, and its criminal quality. These dynamics are a vivid narrative of these experiences: "Frequently when a patient of this kind makes progress in the analysis and wants to change, he dreams of being attacked by members of the Mafia or adolescent delinquents" (Rosenfeld 1971a, p. 174). The vividness of the image of an 'internal Mafia gang' has made it subsequently a technical term for this kind of personality organisation.

Another patient had been in analysis several years, and Rosenfeld demonstrated this coherent segmenting of his personality. One part was violent and omnipotent and had separated off. It sought dominance over a more realistic part that sought relations with people. The patient was keen to have psychoanalytic treatment for character problems, but he showed a characteristic resistance. He often went on weekend business trips and missed part of his Monday sessions: "He frequently met women during these trips and brought to analysis many of the problems which arose with them" (Rosenfeld 1971a, p. 175). Rosenfeld recognised this as an acting out and sought its meaning:

[H]e regularly reported murderous activities in his dreams after such weekends… it became apparent that violently destructive attacks against the analysis and the analyst were

hidden in the acting out behaviour. The patient was at first re-
luctant to accept that the acting out of the weekend was killing, and therefore blocking the progress of, the analysis, but
gradually he changed his behaviour and the analysis became
more effective and he reported considerable improvement in
some of his personal relationships and his business activities.

(Rosenfeld 1971a, p. 176)

There emerged some understanding of the acting out – but why
'kill' the analysis?

At the same time he began to complain that his sleep was frequently disturbed and that he woke up during the night with
violent palpitations which kept him awake for several hours.
During these anxiety attacks he felt that his hands did not
belong to him; they seemed violently destructive as if they
wanted to destroy something by tearing it up, and were too
powerful for him to control so that he had to give in to them.
He then dreamt of a very powerful arrogant man who was
nine feet tall and who insisted that he had to be absolutely
obeyed. His associations made it clear that this man stood for
a part of himself and related to the destructive overpowering
feelings in his hands which he could not resist.

(Rosenfeld 1971a, p. 176)

The man's co-operative self was able, unconsciously to remember
and present a dream. But, it was about the uncooperative resistant
side of himself:

I interpreted that he regarded the omnipotent destructive part
of himself as a superman who was nine feet tall and much too
powerful for him to disobey. He had disowned this omnipotent self, which explained the estrangement of his hands during the nightly attacks.

(Rosenfeld 1971a, p. 176)

This coherently organised split was quite different from the fragmenting incoherence and disconnection of the 'abnormal splitting' in a psychotic state. Nevertheless, it is irresistibly destructive:

> I further explained this split-off self as an infantile omnipotent part which claimed that it was not an infant but stronger and more powerful than all the adults, particularly his mother and father and now the analyst. His adult self was so completely taken in and therefore weakened by this omnipotent assertion that he felt powerless to fight the destructive impulses at night.
>
> (Rosenfeld 1971a, p. 176)

This description of the 'negative ego' makes it clear the patient denied his infantile aggression by posing as superior to all the adults, including his own more adult self. The interpretation seems confirmed:

> The patient reacted to the interpretation with surprise and relief and reported after some days that he felt more able to control his hands at night.
>
> (Rosenfeld 1971a, p. 176)

This reaction was a significant confirmation of the interpretation. It was not just the patient's conscious acceptance, but the actual change in his 'symptom', the uncontrollable hands:

> He became gradually more aware that the destructive impulses at night had some connection with analysis because they increased after any success which could be attributed to it. Thus he saw that the wish to tear at himself was related to a wish to tear out and destroy a part of himself which depended on the analyst and valued him.
>
> (Rosenfeld 1971a, p. 176)

He became more aware of this conflict within himself, and its connection with dependence (on the analyst), an awareness that allowed the aggression also to become more visible:

> Simultaneously the aggressive narcissistic impulses which had been split off became more conscious during analytic sessions and he sneered saying: "Here you have to sit all day wasting your time". He felt that he was the important person and he should be free to do anything he wanted to do, however cruel and hurting this might be to others and himself. He was particularly enraged by the insight and understanding which the analysis gave him. He hinted that his rage was related to wanting to reproach me for helping him, because this interfered with his omnipotent acting-out behaviour.
>
> (Rosenfeld 1971a, p. 176)

The resistance was now conscious and verbal. With more material and detail, Rosenfeld began to demonstrate an increasing dominance of the co-operative side over his wanton aggression towards the analyst who he needed:

> In fact, the patient was moving in the analysis towards a strengthening of his positive dependence, which enabled him to expose openly the opposition of the aggressive narcissistic omnipotent parts of his personality.
>
> (Rosenfeld 1971a, p. 176)

This has proved to be a graphic image useful by many later analysts to understand the difficulties with certain patients who seem to wish to thwart the analyst and his work. As Rosenfeld later summed it up:

> Narcissistic rage arises when a patient reacts to a narcissistic hurt and feels humiliated, looked down on, and misunderstood. It often improves when the patient feels well understood in analysis. In contrast, with the destructive form of narcissism, a patient enjoys hurting, has contempt when he finds somebody loving, understanding, and kind, and puts

all his energies into remaining sadistically strong – regarding any love in himself as weakness.

(Rosenfeld 1987, pp. 22–23)

In taking this step, Rosenfeld had made a significantly deeper understanding of the negative therapeutic reaction that had been puzzling since Freud.

To some extent he supposed a negative side in all of us comes to be organised as a difficult, rebellious and aggressive infant. It is normally under the dominance of a much more responsible self that he can accept realistic needs, dependence and acceptance of co-operative partnerships. The patient lives an internal attack. We often, in common parlance, speak of an attack of nerves, or even bodily problems like an attack of angina or of flu. Such a familiarity with some internal attack perhaps confirms a very common structure of our personalities. Co-operation and community have a very high value in the advance of all aspects of human civilisation, but there is always a pulling back by some other factor in human nature. We have to exhort ourselves to 'make love not war'.

Such states of 'negative narcissism' organised as two parts of the personality in conflict stabilised the early confusion between the love and hate. It has come to be called a "pathological organisation" though Rosenfeld never used the term. It is now found in a variety of clinical presentations of personality disorders, especially those particularly difficult to reach by any form of therapy.

Chapter 6

Borderline personalities

Rosenfeld's analysis of people with relapsing psychotic states included those more stable personalities of which one exhibited negative narcissism. However, he too focused on borderline psychotic personalities where the primitive mechanisms are variable, and draw others, including the analyst, into a collaboration in which their own personalities are directly part of the primitive mechanisms, and not merely representatives of primary objects. These personally strenuous patients tempt the analyst to accept mere symptom relief rather than personality change.

Work with psychotic states, displaying fragmentation, disconnection of thoughts and parts of the personality remained experimental. It is partly because gains made with interpretations can so easily be lost in between sessions. So, the enthusiasm Rosenfeld gained from understanding the early confusional states and primitive means of managing them was balanced by some caution. He advised limits on what could be expected:

At this state of our research we shall not overestimate the therapeutic possibilities of psycho-analysis in severe acute and chronic schizophrenic conditions, because the analysis, particularly of acute schizophrenia, however promising, is a very difficult and strenuous task and the management also still presents almost unsurmountable difficulties. At present

DOI: 10.4324/9781003347590-8

therefore we can only hope to be successful in a minority of cases.

(Rosenfeld 1954, p, 140)

The prospect of psychoanalysis of psychotic states may have seemed utopian, and in fact the work has remained experimental. Its importance however is in understanding related personality disorders and structures which Rosenfeld came to understand as the manifestation of confusional, states or the primitive mechanisms against those states. He persisted with the psychotic 'core' of these problems:

A clearly defined method of approaching psychotic states is important if we expect to do research to clarify the psychotic psychopathology rather than concentrating on symptomatic improvement.

(Rosenfeld 1969, p. 615)

He was clearly concerned that the psychotic core was often missed leading to mere symptom relief. He eventually recognised a broad spectrum of disorders stemming from the inadequate management of early confusion. No longer, at this point in 1969, is the aim to relieve suffering, but now it is research to clarify the psychopathology. However, a lot had been learned about the therapeutic endeavour, and a distinct benefit in working with the borderline states had been gained.

Those personalities present, as he said, a strenuous task. They tend to *use* the analyst in a specific way. Unlike pathological organisations that achieve a stable internal splitting, most borderline personalities 'use' the analyst in a radically different way from neurotics (see Chapter 2). In a psychotic transference the patient seeks to relocate himself or a part of himself in the analyst for purposes of evacuation or control (see Chapter 2). The intrusive quality of such relationships puts the analyst under pressure. This is a very difficult situation as the patient does not just represent the analyst as a problematic figure. The analyst is pressed to collaborate in the primitive processes of splitting and projective identification. The analyst must then manage the confusional entanglements of his own sense of self. This has a direct impact on the analyst. He does not just play a role as a representation in a dream.

The borderline category

The term "borderline personality" was a diagnosis in general use from the 1950s in psychiatry in the USA, going back to the 1930s. It was not such a feature of psychiatry outside the USA. Rosenfeld's background as a psychiatrist may have prompted his use of these medical diagnoses, and he always engaged with US psychoanalysts often using their terms. For Rosenfeld, 'borderline' meant those persons using others for their primitive mechanisms to manage, however inadequately, the primary confusional states. They rarely tipped over into overt psychosis.

Rosenfeld distinguished negative narcissism (as described in in the previous chapter) from the borderline personality:

> The borderline patient who is dominated by confusional anxieties and pathological splitting processes has to be clearly distinguished from the destructive narcissistic patient, as he is unable to face interpretations of a destructive self even if it is clearly exposed in dreams.
>
> (Rosenfeld 1978b, p. 217)

In this later paper, the distinction had become clear. For the borderline patient, confusional states and abnormal splitting contrast with the negative narcissism with the more successful and enduring splitting between a libidinal and a negative ego.

Unlike frank psychotic states, there is enough capacity in a borderline personality for some significant reality testing: "the delusional omnipotent aspects are carefully hidden in reality situations to prevent the madness from being known" (Rosenfeld 1978, p. 218). Reality may be no friend, but it is to a degree tolerated. The fear of losing reality and the confusional anxieties becoming madness seems to require these defences to be very rigid. But they are also very primitive. So, the impact on the analyst of this psychotic transference is difficult to manage, and interpretation can provoke destructiveness. It then destroys the abilities of the analyst, and any benefit the patient might get.

Rosenfeld considered that one factor in this kind of personality development came from an actual early failure or neglect of maternal containing. For a borderline personality, interpretations that are not clearly framed, can then take on a confused form in which a destructive super-ego persecutes cruelly rather than understands. Rigid defences and retaliatory persecution render the patient incapable of insight.

However, there is a sufficiently coherent positive ego which can operate with the reality principle with some degree of validity, enabling less confusion than in psychotic states. This reality may be severely jeopardised in the transference relationship. The "transference psychosis" then degenerates into considerable confusion of positive and negative impulses, as well as self with object (patient with analyst). That may also be erotised with a further confusion of nipple, breast and penis and thus a confusion of femininity and masculinity.

This multidimensional confusion leads to attempts to resolve it via splitting processes to separate good from bad, and objects from self, and indeed self-idealisation from self-destruction. However, it is not a normal splitting:

> [T]his splitting process is not a differentiation or splitting into libidinal and destructive parts of the self, or into good and bad objects: it simply divides the confused self and objects into many different parts of the self and objects which become slices or bits of the confused self and object relations. These pathological splitting processes play an important role in borderline patients, but they are often mistaken for normal splitting processes.
>
> (Rosenfeld 1978, p. 217)

Rosenfeld's characterisation of this abnormal splitting did not translate easily into the clinical encounter, although the patient in the illustration of Chapter 3, "uttered a great number of words" and "he talked about colours", as if the connecting syntax was absent. He may also have implied distortions of sexuality such as masochism he referred to briefly (see next chapter). The early development of the cruel and unforgiving super-ego may be inappropriately erotised as a sado-masochistic encounter.

So, like other severe conditions, Rosenfeld traced the border-line personality: (i) confusional states; (ii) a psychotic transfer-ence; and perhaps (iii) a trauma from early failure in maternal containing.

Early trauma

Rosenfeld was struck by the possibility that borderline person-alities had suffered very early trauma. Without *direct* evidence, he inferred speculatively an early neglect in the infant's need for material satisfaction – the milk. But for the infant, milk is equated with maternal love. He turned to Bion's model (Bion 1959) of the containing mother, with her loving reverie. She provides more than bodily nourishment – she provides an emotional and loving nourishment too. For Rosenfeld, as his colleagues, Hanna Segal (1978) and Bion recognised, this intimate psychical connection is provided non-verbally by the communicative form of projec-tive identification. The infant locates in mother the desperate feelings it cannot tolerate or give meaning to, by screaming and struggling. Mother's loving role is to recognise the baby's state of mind and realise what is needed; "Oh, my baby is hungry and needs to feed", she might say, and will communicate back by of-fering the breast. Thus, she gives not just the needed milk, but the needed meaning to the baby's screams. Known as the container-contained model for the baby–carer relationship, it was extended to the analyst-analysand relationship. Mother's listening and giv-ing meaning is the psychical equivalent of giving milk – and so is the psychoanalyst's.

However, like his colleagues, Rosenfeld recognised that the mother/carer/analyst may get it wrong. The carer may be unable to contain the intolerable feeling or to give it meaning. The ne-glect traumatises the baby left with a meaningless state of mind. It is confused, suffused with hate that cannot be managed and left with the perplexities and dangers of the primitive mechanisms. Above all, the mother has become as impotent with these mental states as the infant.

But, neglect may not be quite so simple as an inadequate ma-ternal container. As Bion originally suggested there may be an "attack on the link". Even when mother does contain the baby's experience, there may be a rageful attack stimulated by the humiliation of dependency and the inability to perform one's own containing. That occurs when, in these early and confused (or later quasi-psychotic) states, the link is attacked by that negative impulse in the baby.

Also, the baby's or patient's projective identification is not always communicative. It may be evacuative, or controlling/possessing. The latter, especially, turns the potential for a containing link into a confusion of identity between the two persons with the creation of an object internalised with the milk (or interpretation) as a primitive super-ego figure:

> [T]here is evidence that borderline patients, particularly the traumatized patients, have experienced long-lasting confusional states [due to persistent projective identification] in infancy and even later on... where primitive envy is excessive, idealization and the more normal splitting of objects into good and bad ones fail to develop.
>
> (Rosenfeld 1978b, p. 216)

The hatred of the need (for milk and love in the form of containing suffering) brings out the confusion of feelings again.

Re-traumatising

This model of traumatic neglect from whatever source – mother or baby – demands that a carer be fully present and listening together with a functioning container-contained link with the infantile experience. Neglect is the failure of some element of this model to link up fully and to give an accurate meaning-making response. Such events happen in an analysis too, and Rosenfeld conveyed it can be a re-traumatising within the treatment.

He gave an example of a young man whose mother was believed to be tense and nervous. She found mothering a burden and breast-fed to a routine acquired from a book rather than from the baby. Despite his accomplished manner as a warm and friendly man, there developed, after a couple of years, a spell of anger and rising criticism of the analyst to the point where the patient decided to leave in a couple of weeks. At that point, facing his leaving, Rosenfeld changed his technique, invited the patient to sit, and then suggested the patient might go through an account of all his complaints and his analyst's failings:

> He was still critical and sullen, but he explained to me many of the problems which we had been experiencing during the analysis. During these exploratory discussions I did not give any interpretations and adopted an entirely receptive, empathic, listening attitude to him.
>
> (Rosenfeld 1978b, p. 219)

Rosenfeld was in effect attempting to supply the experience of a replacement mother that could function quite differently from the narrative in the patient's mind. This was a listening mother who could take whatever the patient threw at her:

> I also examined, as much as possible, my countertransference, for he constantly complained of some tension in me which disturbed him. I noticed that I was not so much disturbed by my failure but I felt guilty and sorry for the patient who had not been able to receive from me what he had expected.
>
> (Rosenfeld 1978b, p. 219)

There was indeed a 'mother' in Rosenfeld that had appropriately received the destructive criticisms of the patient and could in fact transform the experience into a more tolerable form. The demonstration of the analyst's ability to listen receptively and not retaliate seemed to reassure the patient. It had an impact:

> I felt that parting would be painful but, on the last day before he was due to leave, he told me that he would stay with me in treatment and a very pleasant, warm smile changed his sullen face completely.
>
> (Rosenfeld 1978b, p. 219)

The re-enactment of a kind that was different from the early neglect by mother, and different from the seeming neglect the patient experienced in the analysis, had worked, it seems. Rosenfeld's explanation was as follows:

It seemed to me this experience that the patient had projected not only his own feelings and impulses but also the perception and internal image of his mother who could not hold him, into me, and it is this which changed me into his severe superego.

(Rosenfeld 1978b, p. 219)

This demonstrated the replay of the psychotic super-ego actually *in* the analyst as a mother who did not help by containing the intolerable feelings. Rosenfeld had been able to turn the tables and present a listening ear that convinced the patient. A constructive containing link was eventually established – just in time it seemed.

Although Rosenfeld presented this as an example of the complex psychodynamics of a personality disorder, he had gone against his principles of maintaining a standard technique. Reassurance worked by being a corrective experience – the presenting of a containing listening ear – because insightful interpretations were only taken as an intrusion of the destructive super-ego.

Rosenfeld also dwelt on another essential distinction – the problem with this destructive super-ego when the analyst in fact does make a mistake:

[T]he projection of a very primitive superego on to the analyst plays a central role in creating the transference psychosis. The superego seems to have developed in response to long-lasting deprivations, particularly hunger and separations in early infancy and childhood.

{this patient's] transference psychosis did not only repeat the early infantile frustrating experiences in a very dramatic way, but it expressed clearly an urgent desire to find a better solution to the infantile problems with a new object, the analyst. It is difficult for me to judge to what extent the analyst's mistakes or misunderstandings were inevitable, yet contributed to the overwhelming realism of the transference psychosis.

(Rosenfeld 1978, p. 221)

For the patient (and the analyst) there is an overwhelming realism to the transference. Possibly Rosenfeld's technique was necessitated by mistaken interpretations felt by the patient as his super-ego. It then required a 'reset' button.

Chapter 7

Other categories

Having understood early confusional states and the primitive means of coping, Rosenfeld believed he was in a position to understand the complex unconscious processes in various other psychiatric conditions, including homosexuality, hypochondria, depression, addiction, and erotic perversions. These will be briefly introduced here.

Rosenfeld's quest for the deep layers of anxiety and primitive mechanisms led him to explore other diagnostic categories. His method was always to take a diagnosis and investigate its characteristic psychodynamic features in terms of the narrative of a core unconscious phantasy, and to some though lesser extent the impact of his interpretations based on a sensitive verbal formulation of that core. As he summarised:

> In 1964, I hypothesized that mental conflict, especially early confusional conditions (which are particularly intolerable for the infantile ego), tend to be split and projected, evacuated into the body or internal organs, in such a fashion as to cause hypochondria or psychosomatic illness, or sometimes a combination of the two.
>
> (Rosenfeld 2001, p. 24)

Explicitly Rosenfeld was tracing the psychodynamic processes of a number of conditions back to the early psychotic confusional states he had identified at the outset.

DOI: 10.4324/9781003347590-9

Homosexuality

In brief (and see Chapter 2), Freud's very early understanding of Judge Schreber (Freud 1911a) attributed the psychotic state to a regression from homosexual love to a post-catastrophic world emptied of others. This implied a regression to an extremely early fixation point, a narcissistic phase of development prior to object-relations. The self became the focus of cathexis. The thesis was that an underlying homosexuality provoked a catastrophic destruction and an ensuing paranoia. However. Freud's formulation has not stood the test of time, but one element has survived. That element is that reality is sacrificed in psychosis; and was central to Rosenfeld's model of psychosis.

In place of Freud's homosexual thesis Rosenfeld postulated the opposite sequence. Homosexuality, conscious or latent, is a defence against the underlying paranoia not the provocation. The paranoia is evacuated – anally, he said and also identified with the penis as "dirt". Then the penis becomes the instrument for projecting it, and the external object arouses manic libidinal excitement and elation. For instance:

> [T]he attraction to the idealized father is increased to ward off the fear that the father might change into an entirely bad figure, and so into a persecutor. The persecuting father is not only the disappointing love object, but also the rival father of the Oedipus situation, and in addition has all the aggressiveness and badness which is continuously being projected on to a bad object – a process which begins in earliest infancy.
>
> (Rosenfeld 1949, p. 44)

Rosenfeld went into considerable detail in this complex paper, based on four cases. He generalised a process in which both active and passive homosexual relations involve the relation to the penis either as an idealised denial of a bad persecutor or a projection of a depressed and damaged part of the self.

So, the core problem of homosexuality is once again confusion. A confusion between love and hate, for instance penis and dirt. Then by projection a confusion between self and object, and then between male and female organs and identities. This theory

allows multiple individual variations. Indeed, the reaction to confusion underlies all the categories surveyed in this chapter. For
Rosenfeld, transference always represents the deepest aspects of
the unconscious mind, he wrote:

> The anxiety about leaving me and the need for a saw was not
> sufficiently understood in the first session, but it implied his
> inability to separate parts of himself from me. Altogether his
> interest in me as an object is unmistakeable.
>
> (Rosenfeld 1952b, p. 460)

A homosexual idealisation is coupled with the intrusive identification that needs a saw to separate the two parties. Equally, Rosenfeld was indicating that a love relationship can so easily turn into
an identity confusion typical of intrusive projective identification,
and we might include various kinds of heterosexual relations. He
implied penetrative sexual relationships have the potential for
confusional identities, heterosexual as well as homosexual.

Hypochondria and psychosomatic disorders

Although hypochondriasis is very common in a variety of forms
of mental suffering it is, Rosenfeld remarked, little considered by
psychoanalysts. He did however refer to Melanie Klein:

> She has always emphasized the concreteness of the uncon-
> scious phantasies of the infant and has shown that the infant
> relates his physical sensations to objects. For example, phys-
> ical pain may be experienced by the infant in unconscious
> phantasy as an attack by a bad internal mother or breast.
>
> (Rosenfeld 1958b, p. 121)

Hypochondriacal symptoms are for the infant, and at the primitive level, attacks by objects within the body. Mental suffering
is thus split off and projected into the body as *physical* suffering from bad objects; or projected into external objects and re-
introjected as persecuting objects in the body.

   At the primitive level, the objects felt within the self are assumed
to be 'objects' with their own personal intentions. In the case of

'bad objects', they are bad intentions, and therefore experienced is an 'attack' of flu, or an 'attack' of colic, for instance. Good objects, medicines, tonics, vitamins and so on are then internalised to fight off the attackers. So, these 'attacks' of bodily illness have narrative form and contribute to the enduring organisation of the personality into separate (split) parts.

The experience of elements of psychosis in different parts of the body, was according to Rosenfeld quite common:

> [T]he psychotic problems about which one does not have knowledge are solidly lodged in the body organs they have penetrated. A damaging influence is spread by the destructive "psychotic island" lurking in the body organs. The penetrating quality of the psychotic island is linked to the omnipotent projective identification, which has probably withdrawn inside after an attempt at projection into an external object.
>
> (Rosenfeld 2001, p. 25)

This very physical phantasy is similar to the cruel proto-super-ego as a mental structure inside (Chapter 4). However, this becomes a *bodily* 'island' causing physical pain and dysfunction.

Depression

Like many of Rosenfeld's accounts of these various categories of patients, he generously reviewed the observations of other writers from the range of psychoanalytic schools. But he always gave a pride of place to Melanie Klein.

His account of her depressive position was careful, and insightful, and he linked it with his own work on the psychotic confusional states of the paranoid-schizoid position. He could then distinguish neurotic depression (depressive position with reparation) from the more psychiatric, psychotic depression in which he found internal persecution, primitive anxiety and defences. Freud had traced depression to an aberrant form of mourning, in which a lost other person is not grieved over but is internalised as a living internal object.

But Klein described internalisation as a *normal* part of grieving and holding the loved one in mind (in the heart). This, now internalised, object requires care and attention, whilst also often attacked. One form of that care relocates by the attacking destructive part of the self in an external object. Distance gives protection for the internal object(s) which needs the care:

> In 1946, Melanie Klein made further contributions to the understanding of depression by describing the processes by which parts of the self become split off and projected into objects.
>
> (Rosenfeld 1959a, p. 112)

Of course, the projection entails the ensuing sense of a weakened self/ego. Also, that attacking object (now perceived as external) could come home again as an internalised persecuting object – as that super-ego precursor, crushingly critical of the already weak and depleted self. An internal attack on the self has then been substituted for the fear of destroying the loved other person. It is the recreation of a narcissistic preoccupation, although not now an idealised self but the opposite, denigrated to the point of melancholy and suicide. Then, in contrast to the less psychotic depression, reparation can often fail:

> Klein points out that the desire to reverse the child-parent relation, to get power over the parents, to triumph over them in such phantasies, gives rise to guilt and often cripples endeavours [such as reparation] of all kinds.
>
> (Rosenfeld 1959a, p. 112)

The continuing intrusion of the destructive self into even the most determined reparation continues the confusion that destroys the possibility of sincerely putting things right. The splitting also breeds an omnipotent, manic superiority, an idealisation of one's self that no longer needs anyone. So therefore, losing even a loved one matters very little.

Rosenfeld's actual publications allow us to follow the intricate variations of the externalisation and internalisation (projective identification and introjection) in more detail. Here, what is important is that Rosenfeld was describing the close relationship between severe depressive illness and schizophrenic states. There has, in psychiatry, been the invention of the term "schizo-affective" to denote the close acquaintance of the two conditions. He connected both states with the primitive processes of splitting, abnormal splitting and confusion. Where confusion is, then envy is not far behind, contributing to the primitive super-ego figure, external or internal, which becomes persecutory even of good intentions:

> "[That primitive super-ego] interferes with thought processes and every productive activity, ultimately with creativeness" [wrote Klein 1957, p. 202]. This statement is particularly important for the understanding of depression because of the depressed patient's difficulty in using his creativeness.
>
> (Rosenfeld 1959a, p. 114)

Such interference debilitates the productivity in both schizophrenic and depressive states.

Rosenfeld's paper was primarily to display how the range of Rosenfeld's ideas could capture the psychodynamics of severe depression. Although depression may be the combination of biological and environmental factors, he elaborated the important relevance of the psychotic dynamics of a confusional imbalance between love and hate (including envy) whatever its origins in biological factors.

Drug addiction

Rosenfeld's curiosity about the psychodynamics of drug addiction started by trying to recognise why it seems to have defeated psychoanalysts:

> I suggest that the drug addict is a particularly difficult patient to manage because the analyst has not only to deal with a psychologically determined state but is confronted with the combination of a mental state and the intoxication and confusion caused by drugs.
>
> (Rosenfeld 1960, p. 467)

The patient has to accept not just the painful psychoanalytic insights but also the pain of abstaining in a withdrawal programme. Even so, Rosenfeld said: "I found it unnecessary to modify my usual psycho-analytic approach" (Rosenfeld 1960, p. 467). Always determined to keep to strict clinical technique, he claimed in his principled way:

> I feel that progress in understanding the specific psychopathology of drug addiction must come through the understanding of the transference neurosis or the transference psychosis, however difficult this may be, but not by giving up the psycho-analytic approach.
>
> (Rosenfeld 1960, pp. 467–468)

Rosenfeld consistently explored the transference with his standard technique. He wrote confidently: "The drug addict uses manic-depressive mechanisms which are reinforced by drugs and consequently altered by the drugging" (Rosenfeld 1960, p. 468). As in depression, the ego has been weakened, and then uses manic defences. But some ego-strength is needed for the omnipotent confidence of the manic mechanisms and that strength is imported as the drugs.

He described the manic mechanisms as arising in the paranoid-schizoid position to deal with the fear of a persecuting attack, and the disintegration of the self. They include, notably, self-idealisation resulting from identification with an ideal object, symbolised by the drug. By identifying with that ideal object, the self acquires its ideal status, and then a sense of omnipotent control. Such mechanisms lead to the denial of frustration and anxiety, particularly persecutory anxiety. In addition, the bad aggressive part of the self is split off. So, denial and splitting, together with the idealised drug, lead to states of blankness, drowsiness and sleep. The addict blissfully hallucinates or dreams of an ideal object he can unite with, rather as an infant uses hallucinatory wish-fulfilment. The drug acts somewhat as the infant's finger or thumb can be used to assist in hallucinating the ideal breast.

However alternatively, the drug can be experienced as bad and destructive and endows an identification with such a bad object that persecutes the self and others. Then identifying with the omnipotent drug, his haughtiness can allow him to satisfy his destructive desires without anxiety or concern. The effect of this destructive drugging is a considerable obstacle to psychoanalysis, and a worry to all who are concerned with the addict's welfare, because the triumphant omnipotent degradation of his carers makes them irrelevant to him.

The depressive colouring of drug addiction comes from the known deadly quality of the drug the addict takes, thus performing an obvious toxic and potentially lethal act upon himself. Rosenfeld thus added addiction to the conditions deriving from the primitive psychotic confusions and mechanisms. His description of drug addiction ultimately features both the paranoid-schizoid position and the depressive positions.

Masochism

Finally, in a little-known and posthumously published paper, Rosenfeld gathered the problematic phenomenon of erotic masochism into his array of categories that exhibit the psychotic mechanisms and confusions. This paper, not surprisingly connects masochism, or sado-masochism, to his work on negative narcissism (see Chapter 4):

> In many of these patients the destructive impulses are linked with perversions... [Their] power and violence is greatly increased through the erotization of the aggressive instinct. I feel it is confusing to follow Freud in discussing perversions as fusions between the life and death instincts because in these instances the destructive part of the self has taken control over the whole of the libidinal aspects of the patient's personality and is therefore able to misuse them. These cases are in reality instances of pathological fusion similar to the confusional states where the destructive impulses overpower the libidinal ones.
>
> (Rosenfeld 1971a, p. 174)

Rosenfeld illustrated his observations of narcissism with a young man complaining of impotence (see Chapter 5), who told a dream in which a small boy was comatose and dying. The patient did nothing to help; but: "felt only very critical of and superior to the doctor treating the child" (Rosenfeld 1988, p. 152). Rosenfeld took this as transference in which the doctor/analyst was denigrated and deemed inferior to a part of the patient which left the helpless needy part of himself to die. The analysis was characterised by a problem of making real contact with the patient in his negative narcissistic relations with himself:

> The patient felt pulled away from closer contact with me because as soon as he felt helped there was both the danger that he might experience a greater need and a fear that he would attack me with sneering and belittling thoughts.
>
> (Rosenfeld 1988, p. 153)

This description of negative narcissism was then linked with masochism and the negative therapeutic reaction: "This omnipotent withdrawal state is very often filled with exciting, perverse phantasies that produce the constant temptation to masturbate" (Rosenfeld 1988, p. 157). All these states imply a pull towards death, a pull by the negative ego away from help and neediness. It is erotised and leads to masturbation or to sexual enactments of the erotic fantasies.

The core of sado-masochism is an internal structure of the personality in which one part, a negatively narcissistic part, sadistically dominates a needy but erotically masochistic self. The result is a withdrawal, even an autistic state, where phantasies substitute for reality and as noted may become sexualised. One male patient was quite dominated by the following conscious masturbation phantasy: "a powerful Amazon woman – who had a phallus – fighting with him and overpowering him. The woman then forced her penis into his rectum" (Rosenfeld 1988, p. 162). This phantasy was an expression of his personality, split into two between a powerful and destructive negative narcissism that dominates a more accessible needy and potentially creative person. The separated parts of the personality, the negative ego and the more co-operative needy self, come to be enacted externally between two separate people.

Much of this paper dealt with the theme of negative narcissism (Chapter 5, Rosenfeld 1971a), including a further description of a patient who appeared in the 1971 paper. The main point is that there is an internal violence which is seductive, because it gains an intense erotic quality. That quality hides the control, domination and repudiation of a needy dependence. For Rosenfeld, it retains the fundamental structure of an unrealistic balance between love and hate characterised as psychotic and ultimately responsible for the torturing confusion.

The various diagnoses

Throughout his career, Rosenfeld relied on categories supplied by psychiatry. But, despite this he investigated them via single cases, teasing out the very intricate psychodynamics of externalising and internalising the potentially confused impulses of love and hate. He seems to generalise about a particular category when relying on only a single case or two. And so, he insisted that all cases, and thus all categories, can be understood and indeed modelled on the same array of deeply unconscious defences against the confusion, need, dependence and the trauma of neglect.

Part 2

Clinical approach

The conceptualisations reviewed in Part 1 were gained via Rosenfeld's detailed observations of his patient's experiences as he engaged with them in the clinical setting. In Part 2, the chapters concern specific aspects of his clinical approach, and his astute listening to the unconscious experience of his patients' relations with others. Perhaps this is captured best by Edna O'Shaughnessy:

> Rosenfeld emphasises the important clinical fact that omnipotence, however grandiose, is infantile. Beneath or beyond it lies a small lonely infant.
>
> (O'Shaughnessy 1988, p. 100)

Rosenfeld's clinical approach is not original. He started out, with Melanie Klein, to use a classical psychoanalytic technique developed with neurotic patients to work at the 'deeper layers' of the unconscious and research the schizoid mechanisms. This entailed research with psychotic states, focusing still on the point of maximum anxiety and the unconscious narratives in the infantile and transference situations. This followed Klein's method with children and then used with adults which focused on narrative. And its focus contrast with the classical objective assessments of the semi-quantitative distribution and management of energy between the elements of the ego's structure.

Despite Rosenfeld's protestations, for example in responding to Greenson (Chapter 9), there are differences between Rosenfeld's

DOI: 10.4324/9781003347590-10

Kleinian approach and the classical one. It is not so much a difference in the interpretations themselves but more in the pre-
conceived notions of what they consist of, what they interact with
in the patient and what the consequences are. Just to go quickly,
in these introductory remarks, through the specific elements of
Rosenfeld's approach:

i   Interpretations are effective if they address the point of max-
     imal anxiety, and preferably in the context of the transfer-
     ence relationship and the distortion of the reality of that
     relationship.
ii   Interpretation consists of an unconscious narrative 'seen' as
     real, but actually interfering with the testing of the reality of
     others; and it contrasts with interpretation in the classical
     model where needs are coaxed out into conscious experiences
     to be realised in sublimated form.
iii Interpretations are directed to some part of the mind capable of
     verbal representation and communication that can understand
     an unconscious narrative; and contrasting with classical inter-
     pretations that interact with a pre-conscious cathected object to
     enable a greater verbal appreciation of that hidden interest.
iv   The consequence of an interpretation is to acquire a more
     meaningful understanding of some state of mind, and thus
     to provide an ego-enhancement, an additional capacity for
     making meaning of certain experiences.
v   The analyst takes a careful interest in the response to the in-
     terpretation in which some more coherent and less distressing
     anxiety results.

Rosenfeld strongly endorsed Strachey's (1934) recommendation
that we interpret the phantasies in order that reality may be more
clearly addressed:

> Strachey says that it is paradoxical that the best way of ensur-
> ing that the patient's ego will be able to distinguish between
> reality and fantasy is to withhold reality from him as much
> as possible.

(Rosenfeld 1972, p. 456)

Despite his affirmation, Rosenfeld asserted: "it needs extending" (Rosenfeld 1972, p. 456). And he specified:

> Strachey, for example, emphasizes that it is mainly the super-ego which is projected on to the analyst. Many analysts would now add that not only internal objects including the superego, but also good and bad parts of the self are projected.
>
> (p. 456)

More than this, Rosenfeld was aware that the act of interpretation will enhance unconscious phantasies as well as conscious insight:

> He [Strachey] discusses the meaning which patients and analysts attribute to interpretations: to some they are felt as magical weapons, to others they are direct libidinal gratifications which may even become an addiction. He advises analysts to guard against distortions by distinguishing their feelings about interpretations from their reasoned beliefs.
>
> (p. 455)

And interpretations may also be suggestion or reassurance, perhaps not so wholly unconscious, and may thus become a kindly super-ego. That would make the analyst an auxiliary super-ego, which sooner or later will come in contact with other aspects of the patient's super-ego, more harsh and more self-destructive. Rosenfeld's assessment of this potentially complex interaction will be taken up in Chapter 10.

If the mutative interpretation, according to Strachey, is that which pinpoints the immediate experience of the moment, it is not always possible, necessary or advisable:

> Extra-transference interpretations have their place in psychoanalysis, as a prelude to mutative interpretations. However, confusion, displacement and acting out occur when problems which clearly relate to the transference are interpreted outside the transference. He [Strachey] says: it is the task of the analyst to detect the point of urgency when an id impulse is

active: so the interpretations can be emotionally immediate and the patient can experience them as something actual.

(p. 457)

It is perhaps the difference between a patient arriving after a car crash on the way to the session, and a patient arriving for a session after a previous one when his/her destructiveness had debilitated the analyst's mental functioning. At some level, for the patient, there will be a correspondence between the two occurrences. But it may frequently be necessary as a prelude to the interpretation of the unconscious to start with the conscious extra-transference shake-up the patient brings.

As time went on, the challenge to the analyst's own experiences as deeply buried unconscious areas of the mind were exchanged, pointed Rosenfeld to both sides of this engagement. Although from early on he studied his own countertransference, much later he used his increasing supervision of others to study the intra-psychic entanglements of the analyst as well as the patient. He became concerned, as he understood these murky regions, that repetitions of infantile traumas might, and often in fact did, re-occur in the course of a psychoanalysis. The impasse that he noted (Rosenfeld 1987) did not simply show the negative therapeutic reactions arising from the patient's inherent destructiveness. It left a question open as to the relative proportions of the two factors – the patient's destructiveness or the analyst's struggles with that destruction. Rosenfeld's sudden stroke and death interrupted perhaps any possibility of further work to clarify that distinct contribution.

Chapter 8

Classically interpretive

Rosenfeld made great efforts to maintain what he regarded as the classical approach to the psychoanalytic setting and to the technique of interpretation. He was insistent above all on interpreting the transference as it is felt in the present. His writing clearly displayed the principles he attempted to employ.

In a contribution from the floor at the IPA Congress in Paris in 1957, Rosenfeld summarised his clinical approach:

> We interpret the connexion of the anxieties coming to light with the patient's current reality situation and the positive and negative transference, relating the anxieties of the transference situation and the current reality situations to the patient's past reality experiences and the associated unconscious phantasies and memories. We pay particular attention to the interrelationship of the patient's unconscious phantasies and the reality situations, past and present, and we feel that one cannot be understood without the other.
>
> (Rosenfeld 1958c, pp. 238–239)

This extract clearly lists the key points of an interpretation. There is thus a convergence of the unconscious phantasies behind three things: the current reality, the transference and the past reality (as currently experienced by the patient).

We can consider a case in the light of these signposts.

DOI: 10.4324/9781003347590-11

Case: Rosenfeld gave a brief illustration of a session with a young woman whose idealisation of her father together with her castrating guilt could only be dealt with by splitting off an enraging father into, first her bank manager, and then second, her analyst.

The patient, a young and unmarried woman, suffered from anxiety and depression. She had been deeply attached to her father (who was not English) and her disorder started some years after he died:

> On the day of the session I am reporting, the patient arrived more than twenty minutes late, and appeared to be depressed and agitated. She said she had had a terrible shock that day and started to cry rather angrily. Her bank manager, she continued, had rung her up and told her that she had overdrawn her bank balance and asked her to come and discuss the matter with him.
>
> (Rosenfeld 1958c, p. 239)

The shock of the bank manager's complaint suggested more than just an ordinary problem. It seemed that the woman injected a more forceful protest into the scene than had actually been intended.

> In spite of the fact that he had only asked her for a guarantee from a friend, as she had no securities herself, and that this was easy for her to find, she was overcome by fury, anxiety, and depression. She felt that this experience was quite unbearable and she thought she could no longer stay in England. She burst out: "I hate the English, they are all stupid. My father trusted me; he knew that I could be relied upon, that I was honest".
>
> (Rosenfeld 1958c, p. 239)

The woman attributed her considerable distress to the alien quality of the world around as if she were alone surrounded by persecutors:

> She turned her attention to me and said: "Dr. Rosenfeld, you are not really English, are you? You were probably born in

Germany; I do not hate you, you are different from these English, you know you can trust me, you are not stupid".

(p. 239)

So, there did appear to be one contrasting figure in all this persecution – her analyst. She sought his support if possible. But:

At that moment she became more agitated and could hardly stay in the room. She continued: "Dr. Rosenfeld, perhaps you do not disapprove of this bank manager, perhaps you agree with him" – her voice sounded now more sarcastic – "you probably are almost English, having lived here for so long; no, I cannot stay with you. Now tell me: Would *you* guarantee for me? You must answer this question now". She became very insistent and repeated this question several times, making herself ready to leave.

(Rosenfeld 1958c, p. 239)

She needed, desperately, to find a supporting friendly figure who would back her against this alien world:

I interpreted to her that at that moment she wanted to have a guarantee from me that I remained a friendly father to her, in order to keep me apart from the English bank manager, who had become very threatening and frightening. I also showed her that she had suddenly become frightened because I had turned into the bank manager who represented that aspect of myself which had recently been finding out things about her which her father had never known.

(Rosenfeld 1958c, p. 239)

The anxiety was now about trusting this one possible friend who might turn into a similar persecutor:

This related not only to her sexual phantasies about her father, and also homosexual phantasies which we had recently been analysing, but also to her resentment and envy of myself and my achievements, standing for her father.

(Rosenfeld 1958c, p. 239)

In the analytic session the need to separate good from bad was failing:

> I showed her that the muddle which she had been making over her money matters represented a hidden attack on the analysis, since she would be unable to pay my fees. This attack she feared had been discovered by the bank manager, standing for myself. I also pointed out that she felt that in making the money muddle she had actually castrated me, in the same way as she felt she had castrated her father, whose death, in her phantasies, was the result of her castrating attack.
>
> (Rosenfeld 1958c, p. 239)

Rosenfeld was attempting in his interpretation to disentangle the devotion to her father which intermingled with the castrating woman's envy of him which may have been a cause of his death in her phantasy world:

> I showed her that the main resistance was against recognizing the intense guilt and anxiety about depriving and injuring me. To avoid this guilt she had turned me into a persecuting father figure, but this had become intolerable to her and she had therefore split off this persecutory aspect of her father and projected it on to the bank manager while she attempted to idealize me. When this split failed, the anxiety in the transference became so acute that she felt she had to leave the session.
>
> (p. 239)

This long interpretation sets out her attempt to clarify her confusion by splitting the two figures – bank manager and analyst – into bad and good. However, the splitting was difficult as the analyst seemed to change into a persecuting criticising interpreter of her feelings. The analyst's attempt at interpreting was itself a means of clarifying the good from the bad; it may have had some success:

> During my interpretations the patient became gradually less anxious and showed by some remarks that she understood what was going on.
>
> (p. 239)

This encouraged Rosenfeld who reported: "The anxiety about the reality situation with the bank manager then subsided and could be realistically dealt with by the patient" (Rosenfeld 1958c, p. 239). The upshot is that a clear definition of the conflicting feelings and how they are interacting in the session, allowed some relaxation. The claim implicitly in Rosenfeld's description, is that understanding seemed ultimately to be more effective than the splitting defences at this level of primitive experiencing.

The splitting had been an attempt to keep separate the two opposing feelings of love and hate, which otherwise seemed to have had the disastrous effect of killing the father she loved. But we can also address the immediate presentation in the session in terms of the convergence of unconscious phantasies as described earlier – the current reality, the transference and the past reality (as currently experienced by the patient).

> *The current reality*: There are unconscious phantasies behind the reality situation that intensify her fear of criticism and persecution;
> *The transference*: The relationship with the analyst is used to split a good father-analyst from the bad (distanced) father-bank manager to try to prevent the confusion between them;
> *The past reality*: The patient relived, unconsciously, right now, her guilty murder of her loved father.

These add up to the impossible unconscious phantasy of hating and killing her loved father. It proved impossible because the primitive defences did not work sufficiently well.

Narratives in the material and in the sessions Rosenfeld's work presents us with two principles. The first is that there are constant narratives but that one part of a narrative is the avoidance of its inevitability – that is, a defensiveness aims to split and project the bad and the good elsewhere. The second principle is the response of the patient to an interpretation. In a way that is also a narrative – but actually within the session. So, there are two narratives: one that interferes with the meaning-seeking – the transference (and on occasions, the provoked countertransference);

and the other involving two persons seeking an understanding together.

Case: The following sequence illustrates, with a patient discussed earlier (Chapter 4), what occurred step by step. A nurse had placed a glass of orange juice beside the patient as he sat down in the session. In this piece of the record, Rosenfeld was aware that the patient had been physically violent, hitting a nurse on the head when she was attempting to give him a gentle hug. The incident happened at a weekend and the patient was very silent on Monday and Tuesday, eventually uttering single words: "Afraid", or "Eli", and looked dejected. The interpretation had been that he had destroyed the whole world and only God could put it right. Rosenfeld's interpretation had been quite adventurous, based on single words. His own sense of the incident constructed a narrative sequence with an intense emotional content. The patient felt destructive, and even omnipotent. So that he felt unable to put it right. He needed divine help, and this imbalance between what could be achieved destructively compared with any restorative effort made him feel so dejected.

The feeling of guilt was not included in the narrative, so what did the patient's continuing silence and apparent lack of contact, imply? Did the interpretation touch something important and therapeutic? It does not really seem so. Nevertheless, the patient was still coming to his sessions and in some sense being *with* the analyst. So, Rosenfeld seemed encouraged to continue but to expand on the sense of destructiveness:

> After continuing my interpretations by saying that he felt not only guilty but afraid of being attacked inside and outside, he became a little more communicative.
>
> (Rosenfeld 1952a, p. 118)

This interpretation did refer to guilt and to a resulting fear of some punishment inflicted on him:

> He said, "I can't stand it any more". Then he stared at the table and said, "It is all broadened out, what are all the men going to feel?"
>
> (Rosenfeld 1952a, p. 118)

Rosenfeld's further narrative did enable (or provoke) the patient to say more. At first, he confirmed there was something he could not cope with, as if the idea of an internal attack or punishment did mean something. But he then said something more, although it was quite obscure – about all the men. Was the patient encouraged when Rosenfeld understood the guilt and internal punishment?

Rosenfeld had to reflect and digest the comment – broadened out – with a significant imaginative originality, it would seem. This was his next interpretation:

> I said that he could no longer stand the guilt and anxiety inside himself and had put his depression, anxiety and feelings, and also himself, into the outer world. As a result of this he felt broadened out, split up into many men, and he wondered what all the different parts of himself were going to feel.
>
> (Rosenfeld 1952a, p. 118)

Rosenfeld's new narrative clearly resorted to the theory of the schizoid mechanisms. There was both a splitting up process that fragmented the patient's sense of self, and then a projective process which broadened all the bits out into the world outside. It would appear too that part of this is the disaster of the self-damage. He fragmented himself and then placed the bits into the identity of other 'men' somewhere else than his own body. How did this interpretation fare? It may be difficult for any of us to grasp how this experience feels, but did it mean much to the patient? Here was the response:

> He then looked at a finger of his which is bent and said, "I can't do any more, I can't do it all". After that he pointed to one of my fingers which is also slightly bent and said, "I am afraid of this finger". His own bent finger had often stood for his illness, and had become the representative of his own damaged self, but he also indicated that it represented the destroyed world inside him, about which he felt he could do no more.
>
> (Rosenfeld 1952a, p. 118)

So, Rosenfeld's explicit narrative seemed to bring about a much clearer, and literally 'pointed', response. He repeated his previous despair: "In saying that he can't do it all, he implies a search for an object outside" (Rosenfeld 1952a, p. 118). Presumably, that would be Eli, as a divine help. In searching for and expressing the unconscious narrative, Rosenfeld was that assistant working with the patient.

Although Rosenfeld's imaginative narratives seem speculative, they encouraged the patient to express more. Rosenfeld turned to his next step:

> But what kind of object relations do we find in the transference situation? I immediately seemed to become like him and was frightening.
>
> (Rosenfeld 1952a, p. 118)

The clue to the transference, was comparing his finger to the analyst's. It showed how he projected a damaged self into the analyst, and changed the analyst in this way, so instead of getting relief through this projection it continued the punishment, but from outside. So, Rosenfeld wrote: "[He now] feared that he had changed me into himself, and also that he was now afraid of what I would give back to him" (Rosenfeld 1952a, p. 118).

Interpreting the transference relationship brought out by the specific psychoanalytic setting is the hallmark of psychoanalysis. To further illustrate the importance of this kind of transference interpretation, here is a little more material from the same patient:

> The first obvious improvement occurred one day when the male nurse had left some orange juice on the table which he (the patient) viewed with great suspicion. I went over previous material and showed him that the present difficult situation had arisen through his attempt to rid himself of guilt and anxiety inside by putting it outside himself. I told him that he was not only afraid of getting something bad inside him, but that he was also afraid of taking good things, the good orange juice and good interpretations, inside as he was afraid that these would make him feel guilty again. When I said this, a

kind of shock went right through his body; he gave a groan of understanding, and his facial expression changed. By the end of the hour he had emptied the glass of orange juice, the first food or drink he had taken for two days.

(Rosenfeld 1952a, pp. 118–119)

Moreover, this dramatic and visible reaction in the patient's demeanour, his behaviour and his emotional state was not transient: "There was a distinct general improvement in his taking food from that time" (Rosenfeld 1952a, p. 119).

Despite aiming at a classical approach, work with schizophrenic states requires a much broader field of observation:

In the analysis of acute schizophrenic patients the whole of the patient's behaviour, his gestures and actions are to be used as analytic material to a far greater degree than is usual in the analysis of neurotics. The patient often has difficulty in talking and may be confused, negativistic, or withdrawn.

(Rosenfeld 1954, p. 134)

However, as Rosenfeld went on to assert, the general understanding of these observations is classical; that is, defensive features are reactions to underlying anxiety:

In almost all the cases of acute schizophrenia I have seen in consultation or have treated by analysis such typical schizophrenic behaviour was being used as a cover for overwhelming anxieties.

(Rosenfeld 1954, pp. 135–136)

It is for Rosenfeld a question of understanding what that defended-against anxiety is when the patient is withdrawn and verbally monosyllabic and incomprehensible.

Rosenfeld frequently stated that the standard form of psychoanalytic practice takes the narrative from the material that *the patient* gives. It is important that interpretations directly verbalise the patient's experience as he is having it. What then does the analyst use in order to make such interpretations?

Principles of Rosenfeld's approach

The descriptions indicate a number of things, such as its correspondence with the principles set out at the beginning of this chapter. We can see, too, how the analyst finds it necessary to use his own imagination and intuition when communications are sparse. And in particular, Rosenfeld drew on the conceptualisations of the schizoid mechanisms. This imaginative use of accepted theory is commonplace in psychoanalytic work. However, there are also the two important characteristics evident all through this book:

• First is the constant attempt to interpret a narrative process. The interpretations were sequences of different intentions – destructive, constructive, guilt, assistance, and so on – as well as varying locations, inside or outside the boundary (body) of the patient. These narratives were about intentions experienced within himself but also just as often within objects. In addition, there were unstable attributions of ownership of these intentions to himself or to others.

• The second important feature of the interpretation was a sensitivity to the response from the patient. The analyst could gauge the response as confirming or not the effectiveness (and therefore accuracy) of the interpretation. The response may be various, from a relaxation and decrease in danger, to a more explicit communication of the patient's own unconscious phantasies.

Rosenfeld briefly set out his standard mode of working:

> My aim… is (a) to illustrate that an acute schizophrenic patient is capable of forming a positive and a negative transference, (b) that it is possible to interpret these transference phenomena to a schizophrenic patient, and (c) that the schizophrenic's response to interpretations can at times be clearly noticed.
>
> (Rosenfeld 1952b, p. 458)

For many other analysts, such aims are unrealistic. Many have questioned this approach and have experimented with variations and divergent systems, different settings, and with types of interventions other than interpretation. However, Rosenfeld repeatedly asserted, and evidenced: "an acute confused schizophrenic can be approached by transference-interpretations and that a response to interpretations can often be clearly observed" (Rosenfeld 1954, p. 136). So, the success that Rosenfeld was reporting at this stage was: "if our interpretations touch upon his anxieties, we shall get some response. There will either be a change in his behaviour or he will talk" (Rosenfeld 1954, p. 136). It was that increased responsiveness that was so encouraging.

Despite the additional strategies, the classical principles apply:

- The strict preservation of the transference situation
- The understanding that the transference represents unconscious phantasies that have evolved from relations with infantile conflicts, and represent current object relations
- The emphasis on analysis as being an investigation and understanding of unconscious processes *in the patient* which take priority over other kinds of interventions
- The analyst attends to the point of maximum anxiety at the time
- Defences protect against knowing/understanding the pressing anxiety
- The anxieties are displayed as positive and negative transferences

As Rosenfeld stressed:

[W]e retain the essential features of psycho-analysis: namely, detailed interpretations of the positive and negative transference without the use of reassurance or educative measures... [T]he psychotic manifestations attach themselves to the transference in both acute and chronic conditions... The analyst's main task in both acute and chronic schizophrenias is the recognition of the relevant transference phenomena and its communication to the patient.

(Rosenfeld 1954, p. 139)

It had been important for Rosenfeld to establish the effectiveness of classical psychoanalytic interpretations based on the unconscious transference of the patient to the analyst.

However, we have seen in these chapters, on occasions, Rosenfeld did change his approach away from interpretation. One notable occasion was his patient in Chapter 6 who suddenly decided to finish his psychoanalysis in a couple of weeks' time. Then Rosenfeld stopped psychoanalytic interpretations and simply listened, perhaps more in line with the method of Rogerian humanistic therapy. Interestingly this did the trick and the patient at the last minute decided to continue his treatment. The problem had been that through the complex processes of externalising and internalising negative impulses Rosenfeld had been reconstructed according to the unconscious phantasy of the primitive super-ego. Thus, any interpretation had come to be felt by the patient as an unrealistic and cruel punishment. Rosenfeld gave this example of a changed approach openly, and he showed how in this instance a simple listening could rescue a situation which his psychoanalytic interpretations could not. It seems to me that implicitly Rosenfeld assumed the reader would understand that it was a limitation of Rosenfeld at that point rather than a limitation of the approach. In fact, Rosenfeld resumed his analytic interpretations of transference after the patient decided to continue. And that resumption of the interpretive psychoanalytic approach did seem possible though not entirely trouble-free (Rosenfeld 1978b).

It seems important that the setting was sometimes changed and many in a psychotic state were analysed in hospital, the analyst going to the patient rather than the other way around, and at times not using the couch. The patient used the couch when ready. Also, the frequency varied and may have occasionally been seven sessions a week, or for longer than the 'statutory' 50 minutes. As Rosenfeld concluded:

> I do not mean that modifications or deviations should never be introduced, but our knowledge has increased our capacity to interpret in greater detail and with more understanding, so that we can now often deal with severely ill patients by means of interpretation exclusively.
>
> (Rosenfeld 1958c, p. 238)

The example above seemed to direct Rosenfeld's attention to issues much more exhaustively explored in his book, *Impasse and*

Interpretation (1987). What were the forces that led to the changes in his approach? With the patient just referred to, the analyst, was caught up in the role of the primitive super-ego. He had to think about his countertransference, as if that self-criticism had got into him. It took Rosenfeld some time, and a resort to the period of non-interpretive listening to get a grip on this problem between them. Rosenfeld was not completely sure of the problem. Was it a mistake on his own part, resulting from his difficulty in managing his countertransference, or was there was some element of the patient that used Rosenfeld in order to bring out the 'mistakes' that became such a hyper-critical experience for the patient? And so, this complex interaction was explored in much more detail with many examples in the 1987 book.

In his chapter, 'The analyst's use of phantasy', Rosenfeld (2001, pp. 64–73) was alert to certain particular difficulties the analyst may be prone to, including sleepiness, a blankness of mind, and his own 'distracting' phantasies that come to him unexpectedly. He confided a number of ways in which the analyst can consider the depletion of his own capacities. He was aware of how the analyst can jump at possibilities which are not rooted in a connection with what is already known about the patient.

Chapter 9

Debates

Greenson and Gitelson

> Rosenfeld's claim to use a classical approach to the prac-
> tice of psychoanalysis was not accepted by classically
> trained psychoanalysts. Greenson in particular sought to
> dispute this and resurrected the age-old disagreements
> between Anna Freud and Melanie Klein in a debate with
> Rosenfeld.

Rosenfeld's unchanged clinical approach remained consistent
with those of his colleagues working with Melanie Klein's seminal paper in 1946 on schizoid mechanisms. It remains much the
same today. Rosenfeld was open-minded towards other schools of
thought and, unlike most Kleinians after the Controversial Discussion (1943–1944; King and Steiner 1991), he was more willing
to debate with them and to clarify the differences in assumptions,
and to accept the differences that cannot be resolved.

Ego-strength was a common focus for traditions in both the
USA and in Britain. The ego, as Freud said, is the executive
function of the mental apparatus and its condition is crucial for
managing the pressures on an individual personality. In the US,
ego weakness was a matter of incomplete development and regression. In the British (specifically Kleinian) tradition, the ego is
weakened and depleted by an active self-destructive process.

Two of Rosenfeld's discussions have been published, one of a
paper by Maxwell Gitelson and another of Ralph Greenson, both
in the US tradition of ego-psychology. Whilst Gitelson did recognise that after 1946 Klein focused on the actual development,

DOI: 10.4324/9781003347590-12

or disintegration, of the ego itself, Greenson seemed to be on a different track.

On diagnostic approaches

In the IPA Congress in Paris, in 1957, Maxwell Gitelson addressed Rosenfeld's interest in borderline patients, in terms of ego distortion. Rosenfeld offered his discussion from the floor. Gitelson had been at great pains to indicate a huge variance within this category. Distortions of the ego were inconsistent across this diagnostic category. He considered it was a more general dysfunction of the whole personality including id, super-ego and reality factors as well as biological ones. Contending with all that, the ego may not be so distorted but merely held back and "in an arrested state of development" (Gitelson 1958, p. 47).

Gitelson's style was distinctive, as were so many in the ego-psychology tradition. The dysfunction of the ego resembled more the anatomy and physiology of a bodily condition. Perhaps it reflected the fact that US psychoanalysis was then so closely associated with medicine. It gives a strikingly impersonal quality to the descriptions of people's disturbance. In contrast, British analysts, with so many lay analysts, focused much more on the experience of the persons on the couch. As Melanie Klein once said:

> I still cannot answer what made me feel that it was anxiety that I should touch and why I proceed in this way, but experience confirmed that I was right and, to some extent, the beginning of my play technique goes back to my first case.
> (Klein 1959, p. 24)

She observed her children's painful stresses and their repression, and moreover how they expressed them as narratives played out with toys which represent other people and not elements of a mental structure.

So, Gitelson's descriptions had a particular quality, couched in terms of functions, drives and the defences the ego manages. Despite the discussion of categories, Rosenfeld's formulations were in terms of the specific dynamics of experiencing. His formulations were not about structure, but about relations and the narratives of relations, and he tried to exemplify the fluidity of the ego's make-up in relation to the egos of others:

> As an example of splitting in Dr. Gitelson's case one may suggest his patient's way of dealing with his masturbation fantasy. The patient felt no anxiety or guilt about masturbation. When Dr. Gitelson queried this the patient replied among other points: "I don't do it myself in the fantasies".

Rosenfeld is indicating how the masturbation is split off into some imaginary figure, not the patient (Rosenfeld 1958, p. 274).

> It would be helpful to know how Dr. Gitelson interpreted this response of the patient.
>   This and others of the patient's associations suggest to me that the patient had got rid of his feeling of responsibility for the oral sadistic impulses connected with his masturbation fantasies by splitting and projection. I feel that the patient meant to say about himself: "It is not I who am responsible for my impulses, but something else inside me is".
>
> (Rosenfeld 1958, p. 274)

Strikingly, Rosenfeld addressed experiences the patient had – of others or of an alienated part of the self – rather than the objectively assessed ego-functions. Another typical comment of Rosenfeld's was to query Gitelson's assessment that there was no transference for a long time. Rosenfeld speculated:

> Dr. Gitelson reported that the patient asked a great many questions. He also tells us that the patient often asked his father to tell him what he, the patient, should feel or think. I have the impression that this might be a direct transference from the father on to Dr. Gitelson, but, even so, the questioning of the father seems to imply that the patient wanted to recapture his own feelings and his own self from his father which he, the patient, felt he had lost by projecting parts of himself into his father.
>
> (Rosenfeld 1958, p. 275)

Rosenfeld's insight into a possible transference is completely at variance with Gitelson's more classical and 'scientific' under-standing of the mental apparatus. For Rosenfeld, objects, parts of the self and relations contrast with Gitelson's mental structures and functions. Such very different styles were not directly ad-dressed in the dispute which was left hanging.

On technique

Later on, at the Congress of the International Psychoanalytical Association in Paris in 1973, Rosenfeld discussed the paper by Ralph Greenson, titled 'Transference: Freud or Klein'. In his pa-per, Greenson (1974) had re-opened some of the criticisms from the Controversial Discussions in the British Society of 30 years before.

Since the 1920s, Klein's group clashed with classical psychoanal-ysis, represented by the Viennese who eventually joined the British Psychoanalytical Society in 1938 or became emigrees in the USA. The disagreements have been handed down over generations and have settled almost as rigid mythologies about each other. Such disputes will not be explored here. But they remained a powerful set of background factors during Rosenfeld's working life. Green-son understood very well that Kleinians were interested in the problems of ego-development and disintegration, rather than the neurotic (Oedipal) conflicts *within* the self/ego. Simply, Greenson claimed: "The ego deficiency disorders require primarily struc-ture building techniques" (Greenson 1974, p. 39). His emphasis was on deficient development rather than self-directed negative narcissism. This leads to wide differences between Greenson and Rosenfeld – the handling of the transference, different conceptions of the role of actual external others, and what Greenson called an "atmosphere of omniscience" created by the Kleinian analyst.

Not surprisingly, Rosenfeld objected in his more cautious way saying;

> He claims that he represents the Freudian point of view and he describes what he believes to be the Kleinian approach... To understand and present clearly the work of other analysts is a very difficult task.

(Rosenfeld 1974, p. 49)

Greenson had told his audience:

> Kleinians believe they can make deeply unconscious mate-
> rial instantly conscious, and simultaneously render it anxiety
> free, comprehensible and utilizable by the patient.
>
> (Greenson 1974, p. 41)

Rosenfeld disagreed with this: "I would be exceedingly critical
of any analyst, Kleinian or not Kleinian, working in this way"
(Rosenfeld 1974, p. 49). Greenson was working with a quite different model of mental functions. For him, the personality had
diverted its impulses in many directions, many of them *useful* sub-
limations. And so, he claimed that the deeper interpretations of
Kleinians will undermine all such normal development as well as
the disturbed areas.

Greenson asserted: "The Kleinians do not seem to seek a growing working alliance, a slowly advancing active independent coop-
eration from the patient" (Greenson 1974, p. 46). This is based on
a very different conception of the ego, it being an autonomous and
trouble-free instrument of the reality principle. For Rosenfeld, the
therapeutic alliance was not possessed by an untroubled ego:

> A great deal of my work on narcissism relates, of course, to
> the study of the structure of the patient's ego and how this in-
> fluences the analytic process. The analyst constantly tries to
> make contact with the patient's ego, which enables the patient
> gradually to develop an appreciation of the analytic process
> which is the basis of a true therapeutic alliance.
>
> (Rosenfeld 1974, p. 49)

Rosenfeld's target of interpretation was a joint co-operation with
a disturbed, distorted and weakened ego, a self that seeks an alliance. One could say they differed between a focus on id impulses
or on the experience of anxiety. Experience of anxiety was Klein's
starting point with her children and a true difference from the classical method of identifying the drives to be managed by the ego.

So Greenson was more interested in the overall structure of the
personality, and of the ego as the centre of it. For Rosenfeld it was
the fluidity of the ego – its splits or integration, or its movement of
something of itself outside, or back in again. It is as if neither of the

discussants recognised their fundamentally different perspectives and were continually missing each other's point. Greenson saw Rosenfeld arguing for interpretation of the deepest level of a rigid structure. Whilst Rosenfeld said: "I do not concentrate on discovering the patient's most deeply unconscious conflicts, but rather try to ascertain the most immediate anxiety" (Rosenfeld 1974, p. 49).

Though Greenson complained that Rosenfeld had parted from classical technique, it was not a parting at the level of technique. It was a parting in terms of the perspective – the mind as either a functional structure, or as a fluid process of an existential kind. So, the different schools operating from different perspectives and assumptions, may have agreed on technique more than they thought. They shared the primacy of interpretation in practice but conceptualised the impact differently. For Greenson, the ego is assisted in balancing the internal forces; for Rosenfeld the ego is itself the focus of repair. But Rosenfeld did not hold a simple belief in the deepest interpretations. He paid attention first to the point of maximal urgency at the present moment and formulated a narrative in the patient's terms to describe the relationship with the analyst in the session (the transference). Thus, Rosenfeld claimed to gauge the correct level at which the anxiety is generated; for instance, at the level of Oedipal conflicts or at the level of ego integration (or disintegration):

> Analytic intervention at the right level is particularly necessary when the anxiety is threatening to overwhelm the patient's ego and thus disrupt or even prevent analysis. Some patients develop acute anxieties which interfere with the analysis from the start.
>
> (Rosenfeld, 1974, p. 49)

Despite this public refutation, it has not dispelled the persisting contentions that Kleinian analysts are bent on deep-going interpretations diving straight into the deep layers from the very first session. Rosenfeld did not presume to go into the reason for the persisting misperceptions, though he remarked as if surprised on "Dr Greenson's knowledge of the literature and his personal contact with Kleinian analysts" (Rosenfeld 1974, p. 49).

As with Gitelson, the debate was inconclusive.

Chapter 10

Countertransference entanglements

Like many of his colleagues, Rosenfeld worked at a time when the new view of countertransference as a useful tool for understanding the transference was under way. He was foremost in recognising the role played by the patient's mechanism of projective identification in conjuring up emotions in the analyst as the patient needed. This psychotic transference creates complex forms of intimacy provoking existential difficulties for the analyst – as well as for the patient.

Rosenfeld says that at the outset of his psychoanalytic work with schizophrenic states, in the early to mid-1940s, he discovered the importance of countertransference:

> [A]s I realized that my own mind and my own responses to the patient could be a guide to reaching a better understanding, I examined my own 'counter-transference' to the patient much more fully.

> (Rosenfeld 1987, p. 12)

Indeed, he acknowledged his own analysis helped to understand what was going on with his patient, Mildred (Rosenfeld 1947).

We have seen many examples of the need to get a more manageable picture of a person by splitting them in two. For instance, in Chapter 8, the young woman attempted to use her bank manager as someone she could believe was persecuting her, and thus

DOI: 10.4324/9781003347590-13

keep her analyst as a separate 'good' object. Her difficulties were with her persecuting primitive super-ego (or psychotic super-ego, as Rosenfeld typified it). In this case, it is an internal persecuting object, formed in part by the projective identification of a destructive part of herself, then later re-internalised as the cruel super-ego (as described in Chapter 4).

However, a variety of uses of persons in other roles have been described. In discussing homosexuality, Rosenfeld described a man who had become so identified with the analyst that the man indicated the need for a saw to separate the two (analyst and patient). Similarly, there was the man who had a dream in which a German professor (Rosenfeld probably) needed to ride his motorcycle into a gate-post to divide himself into two – i.e. divide the analyst from his patient. These are profound entanglements with real others. They become much more than representing others as transferred objects. Instead, they are fully identified so that one *is* the other. With such a primitive occurrence in the analysis, Rosenfeld called it a psychotic transference.

His interest in this kind of interaction between the intra-psychic dynamics of both parties developed throughout his career. His late book, *Impasse and Interpretation*, is a detailed discourse on this intimate area of psychoanalytic work:

> [D]isturbing experiences created by the patient in the analyst should disappear as soon as the analyst becomes able to realize what has been going on. Lasting disturbances in the analyst take place only if his own feelings become inextricably entangled with those of the patient.
>
> (Rosenfeld 1987, p. 15)

From his first analytic patients, Rosenfeld attempted to check his countertransference when in difficulties, in order to orient himself:

> In treating schizophrenics who have such great verbal difficulties, the unconscious intuitive understanding of the analyst, through the counter-transference, is even more important, for it helps him to determine what really matters.

But the analyst should also be able to formulate consciously what he has unconsciously recognized, and to convey it to the patient in a form that he can understand.

(Rosenfeld 1952, pp. 116–117)

From early on, he recognised the value of his own personal analysis:

When I began to treat a schizophrenic patient by psychoanalysis in 1943 I felt overwhelmed by the counter-transference experiences which caused me considerable confusion and distress. During my analysis with Melanie Klein I gradually began to understand the force of my patient's splitting and projecting processes which I had been unable to observe and understand clearly.

(Rosenfeld 1981, p. 169)

It is the analyst's job to capture these experiences early on and he had quoted Paula Heimann's paper (1950) recommending countertransference as an important tool, "a kind of sensitive 'receiving set'" (Rosenfeld 1952, p. 116), hinting at Freud's (1912) description. The analyst uses his own sensitivity, as a guiding principle but needs to sense both the meaning of the material and his own reactions at the same time:

The difficulty for the analyst to make the exact interpretation which the schizophrenic needs at any particular time is often very great and this applies as much to the chronic as to the acute patients. Our counter-transference is frequently the only guide.

By this I do not mean that we should reveal our feelings to the patient even if he appears to demand this, but we should be sensitive to whatever the patient projects into us by non-verbal and verbal means and become able to verbalize what we unconsciously perceive.

(Rosenfeld 1954, p. 140)

But of course, the patient's reactions to an interpretation are also crucial:

I had continuously to watch for the patient's reactions to my interpretations, and often to feel my way until I could be sure of

giving them in a form that he could use. For example, I was surprised to find that he could follow without much difficulty the interpretation of complicated mechanisms if I used simple words.
(Rosenfeld 1952a, p. 117)

Although psychotic patients may have verbal difficulties, they do understand when touched by something that hits the mark. But the confused identities that typify psychotic states also involve destruction of understanding and meaning, as well as co-operation. Rosenfeld acknowledged the analyst's difficult and subjective task:

[I]t was difficult to distinguish whether the patient made envious, destructive attacks on my mind which interfered with the projective process of communication and with my capacity to understand and 'hold' him, or whether I made mistakes in interpreting and handling his anxieties.
(Rosenfeld 1978, p. 219)

The patient exhibits hatred, even envious hatred, of words and symbolisations in the course of a search for "non-verbal oneness" (Rosenfeld 1987, p. 17) as the work of his colleague Segal (1957) had shown. Interpretations in fact contain many non-verbal communications:

Rycroft stresses that every correct interpretation contains within itself a number of implicit communications from the analyst, such as: I am still here. I have been listening to you with interest and remember what you said now and before. I am not shocked and you are not incomprehensible, etc. He says that the interpretative work of the analyst reflects his interest in the patient as a human being and his ability to understand him. It also gives the patient permission to be himself and have a relationship with another person.
(Rosenfeld 1972, p. 458)

These are implicit communications:

[P]atients respond to our interpretations not only as tools which make them aware of the meaning of the unconscious and conscious processes, but also as reflections of the analyst's state of mind.

(Rosenfeld 1987, p. 31)

And they occur in the opposite direction:

The non-verbal aspects of the verbal communication of the patient are often not consciously noticed by the analyst, but nevertheless enrich and clarify the patient's communication, and may be the vital statement at the moment.

(Rosenfeld 1972, p. 459)

Though we might assume that communication at a verbal level and at the countertransference level need to coincide, sometimes they do not:

For example, while a patient may make a violent verbal critical attack, the analyst may gradually become aware that another part of the patient is crying out for help.

(Rosenfeld 1972, p. 459)

The upshot is a complex communication from split apart bits of the self. How the non-verbal communications are achieved can be difficult to discover: "I came to the conclusion that this process is mainly related to a primitive process related to projective identification" (Rosenfeld 1972, p. 459).

Patients can also recognise non-verbal messages from the analyst, and thereby assess the state of the analyst's mind. That awareness can be used for non-therapeutic purposes – in particular to use the analyst to support defensive strategies, or to engage in a perverse destructive interaction:

It is central to my thinking that analytic psychotherapy can be an enormous influence on very disturbed patients, but this influence can be for both good and ill. Some of the treatments I shall discuss did not end well, although not, I think, because the patients were beyond help. What happened was that an impasse developed in the relationship between patient and analyst, something which can happen very easily with a psychotic patient, and this could not be overcome. I believe that such impasses are often created by the therapist's response to the patient's communications.

(Rosenfeld 1987, p. 3)

He elaborated in general terms:

[T]his positive effort of the patient to recreate a functioning patient–analyst couple (which represents a good mother–child union) is interfered with by his criticizing the analyst very violently even when he begins to understand. This means that even when the analyst is careful in differentiating between the good and bad aspects in the patient's communication, the patient misperceives this. This reversal of roles between patient and analyst becomes now a very frightening problem for the analyst whose countertransference reveals to him what it feels like to be a patient who feels battered and crushed by the analyst's accusing interpretations.

(Rosenfeld 1978, p. 217)

These active intimacies re-enact difficult situations, and the analyst has the job of unravelling the painful situation for both.

But Rosenfeld remained faithful to his belief that understanding in words can still effect important changes:

If the analyst begins to understand at that time what is going on and interprets in some detail that he realizes that the patient had been feeling battered and destroyed by the analyst's interpreting the mixture of good and bad aspects of the patient as a bad part of the self, the patient's complete distrust of the analyst will lessen and consequently the violence of the transference psychosis will decrease.

(Rosenfeld 1978, p. 217)

However, this quote starts with an 'if'. On the other hand, the analyst who does not understand, colludes in a possible impasse indefinitely.

Nevertheless, Rosenfeld confided his surprise that patients can repeat their message in many different ways. They can be very forgiving in that sense.

Colluding and re-traumatising

He, helpfully listed the problems the analyst may introduce:

> [T[here are three issues which have particularly preoccupied me. They are the tendency of analysts to adopt particular directive roles towards their patients, the tendency to offer badly timed and vague interpretations, and the tendency too rigidly and restrictively to pursue a particular line of interpretation.
>
> (Rosenfeld 1978, p. 34)

But he also went on to add the tendency to adopt a motherly attitude (evident in Bion's view of reverie, and Winnicott's primary maternal pre-occupation): "The analyst will be placed via the transference in many roles, not just the role of mother or infant" (Rosenfeld 1987, p. 34). So, we should not be restricted in this way to being motherly – nor for that matter to be the steely indifferent surgeon that Freud described.

Reverie and seduction

Bion had described how the analytic stance of 'reverie' is the capacity to take in the patient's painful and seemingly meaningless experience. To do this, Bion had recommended the analyst must abolish 'memory and desire' in the session (Bion 1967). For Rosenfeld that would deny the human connection, and would demand that we play a *particular* role, defining attitudes, state of mind, etc., rather than allow a role to develop and then understand it.

The relations with the analyst's reverie are therefore complex. This connects back to his distinction between neurotic and psychotic transferences, and thus to the forms of projective identification. In the instance of the patient's projection of hate and destruction into the analyst with the formation of an external persecutor, this cannot be a maternal container in the patient's eyes. That role is a potentially violent object and the patient loses the capacity to see the analyst *as-if* a persecutor. And so to present oneself as a maternal container would feel suspiciously like a denial by the analyst:

> This experience creates a feeling in the patient, not of being accepted or cared for, but of being seduced by the analyst, and on a deeper level it creates a feeling of loneliness and rejection or of being misunderstood. It leads to impasse or worse.
>
> (Rosenfeld 1987, p. 36)

If the analyst interprets the patient's need for an understanding container (mother), it feels for the patient as if the analyst is saying, "You need an understanding mother, here I am". In fact, at that moment the psychotic patient sees the persecutor denying the patient's hallucinated reality, and attempting to seduce the patient's good feelings by claiming good intentions. This form of seduction may of course be temporary, but an analyst may find it difficult to experience being seen as a persecutor. The psychotic transference is too painful for the analyst. The analysis may then fail, as with the case of the man threatening to terminate in Chapter 6.

Collusion

Such psychotic transferences are difficult. It is much easier for the analyst to tolerate a neurotic transference where the analyst can rely on the patient being unconsciously aware, and then consciously so, that he only sees the analyst as if a persecutor:

> [I]f the analyst has many areas which can be described as "private: no entry"… then the analyst and patient may collude unconsciously to keep those areas out of the analysis and so create a therapeutic impasse. The patient may criticize the analyst quite violently in many different ways, but nevertheless avoid the area and the situation where the traumatic experience of feeling rejected by the analyst's behaviour occurs. The attacks of such a patient are often misinterpreted by the analyst, who may try to relate this behaviour to past experiences.
>
> (Rosenfeld 1987, p. 39)

A longer-term impasse of this kind may, Rosenfeld conveyed, actually harm the patient:

> [I]t nourishes his fears that it will be forever impossible for him to be understood and accepted... In these states the predominant patient anxiety is often the fear that he will drive the analyst mad or that the analyst will drive him mad.
>
> (Rosenfeld 1987, p. 40)

To leave those fears untouched amounts to re-traumatising the patient.

One must take account of the remnants of the analyst's omnipotent narcissistic self, which may be difficult to distinguish from the patient's projections, so that we join collusively in representing the needed omnipotent help. If so, the patient will react to this collusion and a complex interaction occurs:

> Severely traumatized patients... are particularly likely to draw the analyst into unconscious collusion... These situations are, of course, extremely painful for the analyst. If they are unbearable to him, the analyst may collude with certain idealized patient phantasies by creating "corrective therapeutic experiences", rationalizing these as assisting the patient in the search for a much better environment or a more comforting object.
>
> (Rosenfeld 1987, p. 36)

Such enactments then destroy the analytic process even though they may help to hide the serious pathology and convey to the inexperienced that progress has occurred.

Some critiques

Rosenfeld argued that analysts are not perfect and will make mistakes, perhaps long-term mistakes, and some critics have accepted this in a simple form. They argue that Rosenfeld by attributing impasses to the analyst's 'no entry' areas and the patient's collusion, was in effect missing the patients' destructiveness, and how the patient was exploiting the analyst's limitations and mistakes, doing so for the patient's own defensive or envious purposes. He is described as looking back to early neglect, rather than the poisonous hate in the patient that exists now:

> I do not think that Rosenfeld would agree but it is my impression that, in fact, he got more pre-occupied with the traumatic factor than the reality of the patient's or child's part in this process.
>
> (Segal 2008, p. 37)

Such a view suggests Rosenfeld had finally accepted the classical notion of a regression to repetition of early trauma, rather than sticking to the trauma and struggles with conflict and confusion now.

As Segal suggests there is room for a debate over the relative proportions of two initiating factors – the external trauma and the internal destructive dynamics. In effect it is a debate over the longstanding problem of discerning the balance between nurture and nature. The concern is that Rosenfeld's central point in his book has the effect of emphasising the actual early maternal (or other) care so that it hides the inevitable influence of the envy that bites that maternal hand of the feeding mother. Segal's concern was that Rosenfeld digressed and over-emphasised the mistakes and traumas inflicted by the early feeding hand.

Perhaps it can be tempting to collude in attributing the impasse to the analyst's mistakes, and leave out the difficult and potentially explosive exploration of the patients' aggressive attempts to exploit the mistakes. It is in any case a difficult balance because the early situation can never be known outside the form it takes in the patient's unreliable memory now. So, the memories of neglect can never be reliably separated from the intricate phantasies of destruction that Rosenfeld unravelled in the present.

It is so easy to accept a patient's reluctance to investigate the difficulties he or she has with aggression and slide away from that to extraneous factors at a temporal or geographical distance, which we can do nothing about. The quirks of spouses, of working environments, of developmental history and of general external frustrations and intrusions are not available for the analyst to change – even if they could be factually discovered. One can only expose the way such patterns of perception are clung to as a template for the present perceptions, including the transference. If indeed there was neglect in the past, that history cannot be changed, only the present exploitation of it can be analysed.

This problematic debate about the external/internal balance led to the suspicion that Rosenfeld may have begun to side with his patients into a collusive blame of others. That criticism may have contributed a resistance to assessing Rosenfeld's lasting influence. It is to be regretted that *Impasse and Interpretation* was published posthumously and so he had no opportunity to further the debate himself about this contentious topic.

Clinical illustrations

Returning to the cases Rosenfeld presented, some his own and some from supervisions, his book in 1987 is a testimony to his astute sensitivity. It is not just sensitivity to the meaning of the material but to the *process* of interaction as the material develops meaning for *both* parties.

Sylvia: In Chapter 3 of the book, he described a supervision seminar in which analyst, Dr M, presented her patient Sylvia. In a Wednesday session very early in the analysis, Sylvia had been unable to open the door after the analyst buzzed it open. Dr M's association was that her own car was not visible outside the house and Sylvia might have noticed. She had arrived five minutes early:

> There was a very short silence, and then she started to talk: "A thing that still worries me is my husband going away. I do not know where it will be, or how long it will be, it may be somewhere very remote, there is nothing definite – and there is nothing definite". Here she makes a long pause and then she says, "Anyway, this is what I am worrying about".
>
> (Rosenfeld 1987, p. 47)

At this point there is some indication of difficulty in connecting. The problem with the doorbell, Dr M's association to the missing car that Sylvia may have noticed, then the material about the husband being absent, described as nothing being definite.

Dr M responded with a straightforward acknowledgement:

> You appear to be living in a state of uncertainty with a feeling of dread hanging over you.
>
> (Rosenfeld 1987, p. 47)

Apparently, Sylvia agreed with this. Dr M continued with her presentation:

> Sylvia replied with something which I do not recall, but I remember my interpretation, namely that Sylvia's anxiety seems to join up in her mind with the weekend.
>
> (Rosenfeld 1987, p. 47)

Dr M's mind dropped something, but she had taken note of the husband's absence, and linked it to the weekend break from analysis:

> Sylvia then said, "It is important for people I am with, whereas at one time I used to make comparisons about how people coped. Now it is the way things feel and how I feel". I interpreted that this meant that Sylvia was very much influenced by her feelings of what she believes other people to be feeling. Sylvia reported, "Yes, I must be very careful if somebody gets flustered. Then I have to be calm".
>
> (Rosenfeld 1987, p. 48)

Here is a conscious communication from Sylvia about the relative states of fluster and calmness in herself and others. There is not a conscious awareness of projective processes of course, but there appears to be a disjunction – at the point when Dr M's mind dropped something. The interpretation linked the uncertainty on Wednesday to the weekend break, whereas Sylvia's response was

not about the weekend, but about the break in the connection between minds over who is flustered and who is calm. Rosenfeld
pointed out this disjunction, commenting:

> Then, when Dr M. started to talk about her [Sylvia's] fear of
> the analyst's absence over the weekend, Sylvia immediately
> corrected her as if she wanted to say, "No, I am not talking
> about actual separations now but I am talking about the
> feeling of loss and distance which occurs when I am actually
> with you, Dr M". I would say that she tries to make clear
> that she is competitive about Dr M.'s difficulties in coping
> with her. She has observed the difficulties which Dr M. has
> in understanding those of her feelings which disturb her,
> and reports this. When Dr M. replies to the patient's very
> personal statement without relating it to herself, however,
> Sylvia becomes more explicit, attempting to say, "Yes, I am
> influenced by your feelings. I must be very careful to keep
> calm if somebody gets disturbed [i.e. flustered]. Like you.
> Dr M".

(Rosenfeld 1987, p. 48)

Although this cannot be called an impasse yet, Rosenfeld was
demonstrating the way in which the minds can diverge and begin
to disconnect. He attributed it to a competitiveness, and implicitly he was interested in the more arrogant destructive negative
ego spoiling Sylvia's actual chances of a fruitful connection with
Dr M. Rosenfeld, described with great sensitivity how this analysis evolved over several sessions. The potential impasse threatened when Dr M. referred to the weekend break – when it was
only Wednesday. The patient was talking about the connection or
disconnection now.

Clare: Another case discussed the inevitable problems that
defeat analysts when the analyst's problematic psychodynamics
are engaged. This patient, Clare, was in once-a-week therapy for
four years with a psychodynamically trained psychotherapist,
Mrs L. This 'thinner' therapy only once-a-week was not immune
from powerful projective identifications. In fact, the impact of the

patient on Mrs L was immediate, in the first session. The patient wanted practical answers. As Mrs L put it:

> The predominating counter-transferential impression was the following: I had got on a train at full speed with her, and neither she nor I was allowed to think about this situation.
>
> (Rosenfeld 1987, p. 193)

Mrs L reported from the initial meeting:

> [T]hings had been amiss between her husband and herself since the baby's birth and that she had lost her appetite and her ability to sleep. Her husband would come home from work at some point in the afternoon, tell her to put on a mini-skirt to excite him, and request her to make love immediately.
>
> (Rosenfeld 1987, p, 192)

Her husband was under the out-patient care of a psychiatrist, and Clare wanted to know what to *do*. First, the patient said: "It can't go on like that. The situation between my husband and me is intolerable" (Rosenfeld 1987, p. 191). Mrs L, the therapist, continued:

> This request was formulated in the register of 'doing': "What must I do?" Moreover, she conveyed an absolute intolerance of the situation and an incapacity to wait and to reflect. The situation presented was one that seemed about to explode at any moment.
>
> (Rosenfeld 1987, p. 191)

Clare continued: "The psychiatrist who treats my husband wonders why I married so late and thinks that I should try to understand why I chose my husband" (p. 191). And Mrs L again commented:

> It seemed to me that she wanted an immediate answer. No postponement was possible; the request for help was pressing. I felt I could either say "Yes" and be caught in the trap of a persecutory situation, or say "No".
>
> (p. 191)

The immediate 'doing' was a pressure on the therapist accomplished as a non-verbal message of great intensity and desperation. Mrs L found herself taking on the patient for treatment without forethought. In effect she 'did' something in response to the pressure – she started therapy. Immediately the patient left that session, the pressure of the projective identification was removed and Mrs L said:

> No sooner had I agreed to take her on as a patient, and no sooner had she left the first interview, than I was faced with a feeling of fright and terror.
>
> (p. 192)

In fact, the situation was resolved within two months. As Mrs L reported:

> Two months later she informed me that she had saved her husband's life. She had left him for some time but when she came home she found him inanimate on his bed. He had just absorbed a massive dose of antidepressant medication. She put down the baby and called the ambulance for him, and he was brought back to life at the point of death. He was eventually hospitalized in a psychiatric clinic and then sent to a convalescent home. At the same time his friends intervened on his behalf. They asked Clare to leave the apartment, and her husband found another woman a few months later. Clare moved to a new house.
>
> (Rosenfeld 1987, p. 193)

The husband 'did' something about the situation, and so did his friends. Rosenfeld went on to illustrate the evolution of Clare's therapy from this immediate pressure of the projective identification. It involved a problem seemingly in the marriage, one where Clare projected an omnipotent child into her husband who had been seriously disabled by the arrival of their actual baby. However, that omnipotent disturbed baby had been re-introjected and its omnipotent demands in full force were placed on the therapist, who had to 'do' something omnipotent to satisfy the impossible demands.

These two cases demonstrate the powerful involvement between the analyst and therapist that must be handled through omnipotent demands of the negative ego on one hand (Sylvia) and of projective identification on the other (Clare). The effect is to put out of action the capacity to engage in reflective work that can acknowledge the felt experience and how it is settled between the parties. Of course, the competitive impact of Sylvia, in the first case, on Dr M's capacity to keep all the connections in mind was much quieter and more hidden than the immediate forceful barrage that Clare aimed at Mrs L.

So, Risenfeld's careful dissection warns us to be aware of who is contributing what, and how such combinations fit, and how each of them *uses* the other. It is so easy for analysts to move away from that difficult dissection and unconsciously fit in with their patients. That then feels like some comfortable success. Bálint and Bálint (1939) talked of the joint creation of an atmosphere in the session, and Ogden (1994) famously applauded the creation of a third object that had significant meaning for both parties. The problem Rosenfeld points to is that factors creating a particular joint occurrence may on one hand be applauded as a joint intersubjective creation whilst on the other are regarded as an impasse. These different approaches need to be assessed against each other.

These cases are a testimony to the importance of supervision and clinical discussion. There is a need for space *outside* the session to grasp the primitive persecution that analysts may have to confront. Not only does the patient have to confront the persecuting inner precursor super-ego, but the analyst also has to confront the remnants of their own inner persecutors. We have to keep in mind a potential alliance between those two – our primitive super-ego, and the patient's criticisms. Evasion he contends is a human mental strategy and appeals to the vulnerable humanity of a psychoanalyst just like everyone else.

The Italian Seminars

Rosenfeld conducted a series of seminars (between 1978 and 1983) for a group in Milan which were published 20 years later (Rosenfeld 2001). There are four theoretical presentations, followed by five clinical seminars with cases presented by the group. The book appears to be highly edited, with much of the group discussion not included. As a result, it is unusually not always easy to capture the flow of Rosenfeld's thinking from the presented material to the fairly didactic meaning Rosenfeld extracted. There often appear to be disjunctions so that a coherent argument is occasionally elusive. This is rather different from Rosenfeld's own writing which so transparently connects his thinking with the clinical material.

The aim of publishing these seminars was to capture this late phase of Rosenfeld's thinking. De Masi claimed:

> [Rosenfeld worked] from the premise that there are some borderline patients whose disturbances are dependent on external rather than internal factors, to the extent that normal development of primary anxieties has been impeded.
>
> (de Masi 2001, p. xvii)

This implies that either external or internal factors operate – an either/or alternative.

In fact, Rosenfeld did not seem to imply this. Rather he can be seen as just emphatically recognising the multiple factors entangled around internal and external influences. It seems to me that Rosenfeld was intent on helping his supervisees understand what a destructive internal world they were trying to deal with. Perhaps it resembles how the patient's primary carers had also been stumped by the negative and dependency-rejecting infant in the past.

Nevertheless, there is a somewhat different style to Rosenfeld's interpretations of splitting and projective identification at this late stage. This is almost certainly because some cases he discussed were not so severe as the acute psychotic states he described from the 1950s. Rosenfeld was trying to emphasise what he had learned about the intensity of the psychotic transference, and the analyst's difficulties in holding on to what is happening to him/herself, as well as to the patient. This was in fact Rosenfeld's gift. If Bion's assertion was that the analyst has to keep thinking whilst under fire, Rosenfeld was one analyst, *par excellence*, who accomplishes that – often. He seemed intent to pass on his discoveries of how easy it is to fail as an analyst by not grasping the intense negativity towards the analyst, and the patient's negativity and destructiveness towards himself.

Whilst Rosenfeld may seem at times to admonish the analyst, he is also sensitive to the intense negative pressures such patients struggle with, and impose on their analysts:

> It is only by understanding our problems, difficulties, and failures in treating schizophrenia and other psychotic conditions that we can gradually achieve greater successes.
>
> (Rosenfeld 2001, p. 23)

Learning from one's failures means facing the destructiveness, anxiety and persecution it causes, whilst not forgetting that it is the libidinal reality-oriented ego that is persecuted by its own negativity. It became Rosenfeld's concern, that an unwitting re-traumatising can result for some unfortunate people we had wished to help, and who we therefore fail. With his own difficult life experiences, Rosenfeld may have felt a special need to help analysts who consciously or unconsciously hesitate with those painful destructive and punitive impulses that so disturb the patient.

That something has gone wrong for the patient in the past may be undeniable, but the patient tells the story with his defences intact:

> [W]e may ascribe too much significance to the presentation of history, as it is told, thereby failing to recognize the importance of other things and of failing to recognize that the patient has defended him/herself from problems of a different origin, attributing them exclusively to external events.
>
> (Rosenfeld 2001, p. 78)

This kind of slippage from the immediate painful destructiveness to a collusive blaming of the past is a constant temptation. Rosenfeld's encouragement to constantly point gently to the living moment in the room, can only slowly bring out from behind the defences, the proper connections with what the patient needs to have understood in himself, however shocking.

After-thoughts
Reflections on a life's work

Rosenfeld's smile and his gentleness seemed to contrast with the violence of the material he exposed in his patients and supervisees. However, he had a strong conviction of what he thought, and he saw himself as presenting an authoritative opinion. He was a settled family man, living in an affluent part of London with a large athletic physique he devoted to playing tennis. It almost seems incongruous that he also had a passion for what seems like the opposite in his patients and in his work. He was extremely alert to the lobbing back and forth of aspects of a person's self, like the ball in a tennis match; as well as the destructiveness behind that murderous competitiveness.

It is not clear why such a calm and composed man would spend a lifetime diving deep into the worst of troubles that can beset humankind. It is the case that his life had not always been serene, and he had experienced the anxious disruption of Nazi antisemitism which required his emigration and the disruption of his family. Subsequently his immigrant status was unsettled and must have been insecure for some years during the Second World War; and it is possible this left a haemorrhaging scar beneath the surface of his personality. He left almost no published material on his personal life and beliefs, and he appeared totally focused on the biographies and lives of others. Some more surface details of his life were collected by his daughter. And she too was not acquainted with any sense of struggle during this difficult period for her father: "It must have been both traumatic and devastating. I do not know who, if anyone, he spoke to about his experiences or how he and my mother dealt with them" (Rosenfeld 2016, p. 223). His daughter also remarked: "He was so present yet so unavailable" (Rosenfeld 2016, p. 228), and this remains something of a mystery that there is such an intense depth of understanding in Rosenfeld, and yet a screen is thrown across that strong presence.

His analysis with Melanie Klein has a profound connection. Klein's schizoid mechanisms described in 1946, appear as the bedrock of Rosenfeld's thinking throughout his career. Indeed, it is almost as if during his analysis with Klein, and his own work with Mildred, prior to Klein's paper, they were working jointly on those conceptions. In fact, his analysis of Mildred pointed Rosenfeld in a completely parallel direction, that it almost challenged Klein's leadership. So, when she was about to publish her paper; "[S]he asked him very sweetly if he would mind postponing his presentation of his paper until she had delivered the one she was preparing" (Grosskurth 1986, p. 372). Rosenfeld in his unassuming way complied, and his own paper describing his findings with Mildred was published one year after hers, in 1947. In fact, this collaboration could bring to mind Rosenfeld's account of the possible confusion of identity between analyst and analysand.

Increasingly from about 1978, Rosenfeld addressed the strain on the analyst's own experiences of being used. At the time Rosenfeld was writing *Impasse and Interpretation*, others were investigating the union of patient and analyst as a joint intersubjective creation; for instance, Stolorow, Atwood and Ross (1978), Stolorow and Atwood (1984) and Brandchaft (1986). Though Rosenfeld would have been aware of such writing, he made no reference to these significant writers or to the new schools of psychoanalysis, although he did note the previous generation of Freda Fromm-Reichman and Harold Searles.

Despite Rosenfeld's detailed investigations of the interpersonal entanglements within a psychoanalysis, he was not interested in how such joined worlds might be relevant to the context of community and social cultures in which we all live and adapt. That seemed to be something left to the reality principle in everyone and he expressed no interest in group dynamics despite the nationalism from which he himself had suffered. Nevertheless, the pressing fact is that a person helps to construct the world he lives in – we are our own context as we meet with others contributing to our own context. This is complex, but to my mind should have interested him at a social level. His life had been dislocated by powerful social forces, but it seems he never considered the events of his homeland in the 1930s worth putting to paper.

Glossary

NOTE: Much of this glossary refers to terms in general use within the Klein group as a whole, of which Rosenfeld was a central and orthodox figure. The specific terms which he is responsible for introducing or developing are indicated in **bold print**.

Abnormal splitting
Normal splitting (see also *Idealisation*, and *Primitive processes*) divides others into good and bad objects with regard to their intentions towards the subject. Abnormal splitting occurs at a very early stage to attempt a separation and reduce confusion by arbitrarily assigning the good-bad distinction to self and others. That more random assignment then idealises (or demonises) others irrespective of their actual characteristics. It may especially occur where there is a difficulty in making the distinction, for instance when a carer is also an abuser. However, it applies to many conditions where normal splitting is difficult or fails as an adequate defence.

*****

Borderline personalities
The term "borderline personality" was coined in psychiatry in the USA. Rosenfeld was responsible for bringing the term into specific use in British psychoanalysis because of its relevance in working with psychotic states, and those personalities which depend especially on the primitive mechanisms. The

term brings them close to psychosis but preserves a greater functioning of the reality principle at the same time (see also *Pathological organisation of the personality*).

*****

Classical interpretation

Rosenfeld argued consistently that his method of interpretation continued the classical model. However, there do seem to be necessary differences. Although the aim is some understanding of the unconscious anxiety and the defences, the target tends to be different. The approach of classical analysts is to offer some sort of auxiliary ego, but one which assists the ego to manage and to sublimate drives which have been blocked in their primitive form. The personal is encouraged to start with the derivatives and work back step by step to the unconscious sources behind the derivatives. Drawing energy from the unconscious to the preconscious and ultimately to make it conscious results in a more acceptable (sublimated) creativity. Rosenfeld, as a Kleinian, sought to address the anxiety – the "point of urgency" – in each session. If the analyst can face the anxiety it is some sort of learning for the patient to manage to do so too. Two heads are better than one.

*****

Confusional states

Rosenfeld described how difficult an infant must find it to sense of the very earliest experiences after birth. The crucial emotions of love and hate are not easily kept distinct. They become confused with each other in a frantic state of mixed-up feelings. The infant adopts various means to separate them including the use of the ego boundary by locating some emotional experiences outside the self. Such a method of projecting an aspect (either hating or loving) outside the self leads to a comparable confusion of identity between the self and the object projected into.

Keeping the separate emotions clearly defined and especially the love kept from being confused with hate is a major developmental achievement. This tussle for emotional stability and dominance of love is close to the general Kleinian view of a mature development. There is a superficial resemblance to what Freud called the fusion and defusion of the life and death instincts. But for Freud fusion often represented a creative combination, not confusion and ultimately sublimation at later stages of development.

*****

Death instinct

Like most of the Klein group. Rosenfeld used the term "death instinct" to represent an inherent destructive response towards others and the self. Both the libido and the death instinct denote narrative unconscious phantasies in response in object-relations. Whereas libido is a response to a life-giving object that satisfies demands, the death instinct is manifest in response to a persecuting frustration of needs or an envious hatred of dependence on more resourceful others. Frequently Rosenfeld, for simplicity, used the terms love and hate, though the intention is to refer to something rooted as much in bodily demands that are satisfied of frustrated.

*****

Depersonalisation

Mildred, Rosenfeld's first patient with psychotic features, impressed him with her tendency to feel lost or blank, as if aspects of her personality just went missing. Indeed, they did go missing in the sense that the ego split off parts and functions that threatened or caused severe anxiety, leaving a felt emptiness as a person – depersonalised. This work prior to Melanie Klein's paper on schizoid mechanisms in 1946, could then be seen in terms of those mechanisms – splitting and projection of parts of the self (known from 1952 as "projective identification"). Thereafter, Rosenfeld dropped the term although it is still an apt description of many psychotic states (see *Projective identification*).

*****

Ego

The ego is seen in psychoanalysis as the executive part of the personality, although for Rosenfeld and Klein it is not really distinguishable from the idea of self. Freud's metaphor of the apparatus of id/ego/super-ego was borrowed by the Kleinians but it was not so precise and the functions of the mind were actually experienced as relations between internal entities, objects or parts of the self, including the super-ego as a special internal object concerned with morality and punishment. Importantly, the self, from the outset, includes a boundary separating it from the external world, and useable for defensive or reality purposes (see *Self*).

*****

Envy

Envy has been a debating point between Kleinians and classical psychoanalysts for many years. It is a significant and painful experience which brings together love and aggression in anxiety-provoking ways. For Rosenfeld, it seriously complicates the sorting out of the confusion of feelings from the outset. The provoking cause is a humiliating dependency on others who are more resourceful. The early omnipotent ego is provoked to hate and to destructiveness against those others that can provide and are seen as omnipotent instead.

*****

Idealisation

The early problems of keeping hate from interfering with love often entailed characterising some person as completely ideal and only loved. Another person then existed somewhere to be hated for their demonic and persecutory nature. Other persons are from the beginning seen in this way as having either of these intentions towards the subject and are attributed with having a mind themselves. Despite this careful and rescuing division, it rarely accords with reality and has slowly to be set aside in the course of development, with an acknowledgement that no one is perfect (nor anyone all bad) – an achievement of reality known as the depressive position (see *Omnipotence*).

*****

Libidinal phases

Rosenfeld made use of these classic psychoanalytic concepts and terms such as oral, anal and genital, despite the fact that they often seem to clash with the concepts and terms of the Klein group he adhered to. It was not just a diplomatic device since his use of 'libido', was not quite the same. For Rosenfeld, the tactile sensitivity of the three orifices was incorporated into the unconscious phantasies of expelling or internalising parts of the person's own self or those of other objects. They had less relevance to erotic satisfactions and more as defences against anxieties. They were also not necessarily a developmental sequence and different personalities use one rather than another as appropriate for the primitive defences of projection and introjection. Rosenfeld's accounts rarely refer to the sites of instinctual stimulation, but feature as the general dramas of splitting and redistribution of the self and internal objects that are good or bad (see *Primitive processes*).

*****

Negative narcissism

Whilst Freud described narcissism as self-love when the libido turns towards the self/ego exclusively and excludes others, in line with the classical Greek myth of Narcissus, Rosenfeld considered a similar turning of the aggressive impulses towards the self. Self-hate is not uncommon. It has various forms but notably it can be seen as a core of a psychotic state which destroys the part of the self that acknowledges reality. In addition, it can prompt a more stable personality that is pathologically organised around a split into negative and positive parts of the ego in the same person. When the balance goes towards the negative, it can manifest as bodily self-harm and suicide as well as psychic splitting (see also *Pathological organisation of the personality*).

*****

Oedipus complex

Following Melanie Klein, Rosenfeld accepted that in most instances the difficulties in managing the conflicts of the Oedipus complex result from difficulties and distortions that lie beneath and result from an ego incapable of resolving conflicts. The 'deeper layers' of trouble and disturbance arise from a defective development of the ego which has not adequately dealt with the conflicts and confusions of love and hate, and has resisted developing the functions of conflict-resolution ever after. The challenges of the Oedipus complex will only be coped with once the ego is coherent and functional, but the complex still threatens the confusion of love and murder.

*****

Omnipotence

Omnipotence is an assumed attribute of one's self. It has a defensive function in protecting against painful experiences connected with separateness, dependence and need, and therefore defends against neglect, uncertainty and also envy. The reality of the need for others is repudiated in early development, and results in persisting difficulties when self-satisfaction is the goal. It is a feature of the reality-defying negative ego to be found in *Pathological organisations of the personality*.

*****

Pathological organisations of the personality

Perhaps the most used of Rosenfeld's contributions to psychoanalysis is his understanding of the stable organisation of the self into a positive and a negative ego. They engage in a continual battle for dominance within the personality. In particular, a strong negative ego continually submits the positive ego to a crushed invisibility and the result is a person who tends to be hard, indifferent, unappreciative of warmth and help and seemingly omnipotently without need of anyone. Gratitude, consideration and help appear to be outside the range of such people. However, on psychoanalytic examination there is a warmer and vulnerable side which is kept shamefully hidden and disowned. Power and weakness pre-occupy the attention in all the dealings of such personalities. This kind of dominance of a negative ego is often known as the "inner mafia gang".

*****

Primitive processes

Primitive defence mechanisms operate to manage confusional states where love and hate are not at first fully distinguished, and also when they are distinguished they protect the love and the loved one from hate. Central is a splitting of the self/ego as a self-inflicted division of the person into good parts and bad ones; and secondly it divides others into good objects and bad ones.

Splitting off functions and experiences leaves an apparent blankness of affect and interest. It is quite different from repression, where there is no blankness or conscious loss of awareness because substitute representations are employed, as in dreams. Splitting off crucial functions gives a remarkable self-awareness of loss, of being out of joint and indifferent, leading to Klein's seminal paper in 1946.

In combination with splitting there are a number of other mechanisms that support the splitting of the ego. These include relocating parts into the external world and into others, or locating parts of others within themselves, including specific bodily locations. For Rosenfeld, and an increasing number of psychoanalysts today, projective identification is a singularly important mechanism which creates confused identifications with other persons, sometimes felt metaphorically and sometimes very concretely.

Splitting of the self into good and bad inevitably leads to others felt to be objects that are uniquely good or bad, ideal or persecutory (idealised or demonised) depending on the nature of the part split from the self (see *Idealisation*; *Projective identification*).

*****

Projective identification

Following splitting of the self, separated parts may be located, in the being of someone else. Despite this being 'in phantasy', it is nevertheless felt to be concretely actually within another person and active there. This creates the other as in some singular way connected with the projecting subject. Rosenfeld described three forms of projective identification – first, an evacuation of some bad part of the self in order to rid the self, thus 'purifying' it and making it more ideal; second, a communication to another person of some particular state of mind, usually one that it is intolerable by being meaningless, or extremely threatening in some other way; and third, entering another person with the intention to take them over and possess them in an act of power or ownership. Other forms of projective identification have been described by other psychoanalysts (see *Primitive processes*).

*****

Psychotic transference

Rosenfeld described how the transferences from people in psychotic states are quite distinct from those at a neurotic level. In psychosis, patients do make a transference right from the initial contact but employ the unconscious phantasies of the primitive mechanisms of splitting, projection and

introjection, and issues of identification. In contrast a neurotic transference uses the analyst as a representation of some
other significant object, however distorted by regression, displacement and condensation. The psychotic transference is
not a representation but is felt to fundamentally remould the
identity of self and other (see *Primitive processes*).

*****

Reality principle

Freud discovered his account of the reality principle and its six
component functions when attempting to understand Judge
Schreber's psychosis. Schreber was psychotic, characterised
as most psychiatrists agree with a rejection of reality. The
particular functions needed for the reality principle, are:
consciousness of sense perception, attention to particular
percepts, judgement about whether they are true or false, a
notation for memorising the results of these functions, the
inhibition of motor action that responds to a stimulus, and
the substitution of thought in the space created by the inhibition, leading to thinking as a form of experimental action.
Most psychoanalysts working with people in psychotic states
accept these functions, or some of them, as out of action.
Rosenfeld, in the Klein group, regarded the dismantling of
the reality principle as an act of self-destructiveness aimed at
avoiding the frustration of some real stimulus including the
arousing of envy (see *Envy*; *Confusional states*).

*****

Regression

Rosenfeld only occasionally made reference to regression. He did
however use this term in discussion with more classical analysts who regarded the build-up of tension to be managed
by regressing to earlier stages of development. Rosenfeld
however envisaged constantly active unconscious phantasy
throughout life arising from the paranoid-schizoid position
and its specific anxiety and primitive mechanisms of defence.

So, a retreat to a more psychotic experience of others as violent persecutors is an experience of ordinary people. After all,
it would not be possible for ordinary soldiers to fight a war
without the facility to slot into the kill-or-be-killed mode of
thinking. However, in unconscious phantasy, it could become
stabilised as a psychotic state or a psychotic transference.

Regression is therefore to deeper unconscious levels, rather than to
the past. As with Klein, regression conforms more to Freud's
notion of the topological form rather than the temporal one.

*****

Self

The Klein group tended to use the terms "self" and "ego" inter-
changeably, often preferring the term 'self' as it seems more
experiential. The self has more in common with the Ger-
manic 'Ich' which Freud used, than the scientific tone of 'ego'.
Having said that, Rosenfeld did invariably use the term 'ego',
probably out of respect for good relations between schools.
However, there is, like so many terms used in common across
psychoanalytic schools, a different nuance of meaning as it
crosses the boundaries. In the classical tradition, 'ego' acquired a very specific meaning as the executive function in
the apparatus of the mind dealing with the accumulation of
stimuli and their satisfaction or sublimation (or, in contrast,
their defensive repression). For Rosenfeld, there is not such a
precise meaning and self is meant to indicate a person's experience, their sense of themselves. It is not just a manager of
the energic needs but is a narrative player amongst objects.
The self is also extraordinarily fluid being able to divest itself
of certain parts and functions which contribute to intolerable
anxieties (see *Ego*; *Primitive processes*).

*****

Super-ego

Rosenfeld made a discovery very early on in his work with psychosis. He knew that there was a dispute within psychoanalysis

that had been unsettled for 20 or more years. concerning the origins and development of the super-ego. Freud view it as the "heir to the Oedipus complex". But on clinical evidence, Klein disputed that. She categorically asserted that a super-ego exists in the development of a child a long time before the Oedipus complex resolves, and so its basis is from some other source. Rosenfeld entered this debate by tracing the origins or precursors back to the very primitive levels of function that can be observed in the psychotic mind. As noted in Chapter 4, Rosenfeld redrew Freud's understanding of psychosis; rather than Freud's view that Schreber denied the reality of his own homosexual attraction to his doctor and became paranoid, Rosenfeld said Schreber was paranoid and it gave rise to defensive formations involving homosexuality. So, Rosenfeld thought that his contribution could be the understanding of the primary status of paranoia. And similarly for the super-ego; its earliest manifestation (or precursor) is the product of early paranoia which gives it such a harsh quality. The need in early infancy to deal with the confusion and conflict between love and hate is resolved by projecting hatred, and the hating part of oneself into an external object, which thereby becomes a persecuting menace. The next step is this hostile object can intrude its way back into the interior of the subject, creating an internal structure, critical and punitive towards the self that had originally projected it.

Guilt, which is the core anxiety of the depressive position, comes from the recognition of the reality of the co-existence of love and hate towards the one person – hating the needed loved one. This therefore means the super-ego develops from being an intensely persecuting precursor of the conscience to becoming a more benign, maybe forgiving, inspiration for doing good, for the success of love over hate, and for the repair of any damage done to loved ones. This sequence of development is quite obviously different from the classical model. For Rosenfeld the important point is that love-versus-hate is managed by the to-and-fro of projection and introjection.

*****

Transference psychosis
(see *Psychotic transference*)

*****

Unconscious phantasy
Whilst in Rosenfeld's lifetime, classical psychoanalysis investigated the way instincts are handled by the executive ego, the object-relations tradition give experiences a narrative form. So, love and satisfaction are felt unconsciously as being loved by someone who intends to satisfy and sustain one's life, whilst frustration and hate are felt as resulting from someone intending to harm. Instincts in fact are felt as unconscious phantasies. Thus unconscious phantasies are narrative experiences that exist in the unconscious (like dreams). They are not quantitative distributions of instinctual energy. When awake they are not consciously known, despite of course unconsciously interfering with conscious thoughts and feelings as if they are real narratives.

Publications of Herbert Rosenfeld

1 Rosenfeld, H. (1947) Analysis of a schizophrenic state with depersonalization. *International Journal of Psychoanalysis* 28: 130–139. Reprinted 1965 in *Psychotic States*: 3–27. London: Hogarth Press.

2 Rosenfeld, H. (1949) Remarks on the relation of male homosexuality to paranoia, paranoid anxiety and narcissism. *International Journal of Psychoanalysis* 30: 36–47. Reprinted 1965 in *Psychotic States*: 34–51. London: Hogarth Press.

3 Rosenfeld, H. (1950) Note on the psychopathology of confusional states in chronic schizophrenias. *International Journal of Psychoanalysis* 31: 132–137. Reprinted 1965 in *Psychotic States*: 52–62. London: Hogarth Press.

4 Rosenfeld, H. (1952a) Notes on the psycho-analysis of the superego conflict of an acute schizophrenic patient. *International Journal of Psychoanalysis* 33: 111–131. Reprinted (1955) in M. Klein, P. Heimann and R. Money-Kyrle (eds.) *New Directions in Psychoanalysis*: 180–219. And reprinted (1965) in *Psychotic States*: 111–131. London: Hogarth Press.

5 Rosenfeld, H. (1952b) Transference phenomena and transference analysis in an acute catatonic schizophrenic patient. *International Journal of Psychoanalysis* 33: 457–464. Reprinted (1965) in *Psychotic States*: 104–117. London: Hogarth Press.

6 Rosenfeld, H. (1954) Considerations regarding the psychoanalytic approach to acute and chronic schizophrenia. *International Journal of Psychoanalysis* 35: 135–140. Reprinted (1965) in *Psychotic States*: 117–127. London: Hogarth Press.

7 Rosenfeld, H. (1958a) Discussion on ego distortion. *International Journal of Psychoanalysis* 39: 274–275.

8 Rosenfeld, H. (1958b) Some observations on the psychopathology of hypochondriacal states. *International Journal of Psychoanalysis* 39: 121–124.

9 Rosenfeld, H. (1958c) Contribution to the discussion on variations in classical technique. *International Journal of Psychoanalysis* 39: 238–239.

10 Rosenfeld, H. (1959a) An investigation into the psycho-analytic theory of depression. *International Journal of Psychoanalysis* 40: 105–129.

11 Rosenfeld, H. (1959b) Envy and gratitude: A study of unconscious forces: By Melanie Klein. *International Journal of Psychoanalysis* 40: 64–66.

12 Rosenfeld, H. (1960) On drug addiction. *International Journal of Psychoanalysis* 41: 467–475. Reprinted (1965) in *Psychotic States*: 128–143. London: Hogarth Press.

13 Rosenfeld, H. (1962a) The superego and the ego-ideal. *International Journal of Psychoanalysis* 43: 258–263.

14 Rosenfeld, H. (1962b) Review of *Psychotherapy of the Psychoses*. Edited by Arthur Burton. New York: Basic Books, 1961. *International Journal of Psychoanalysis* 43: 184–188.

15 Rosenfeld, H. (1964a) The psychopathology of hypochondriasis. Reprinted (1965) in *Psychotic States*: 180–199. London: Hogarth Press.

16 Rosenfeld, H. (1964b) On the psychopathology of narcissism: A clinical approach. *International Journal of Psychoanalysis* 45: 332–337. Reprinted (1965) in *Psychotic States*: 169–179. London: Hogarth Press.

17 Rosenfeld, H. (1969) On the treatment of psychotic states by psychoanalysis: An historical approach. *International Journal of Psychoanalysis* 50: 615–631.

18 Rosenfeld, H. (1971a) A clinical approach to the psychoanalytic theory of the life and death instincts: An investigation into the aggressive aspects of narcissism. *International Journal of Psychoanalysis* 52: 169–178.

19 Rosenfeld, H. (1971b) Contribution to the psychopathology of psychotic patients: The importance of projective identification in the ego structure and object relations of the psychotic patient. In Bott Spillius, E. (1988) *Melanie Klein Today: 1. Mainly Theory*: 117–137. London: Routledge. Previously published (1971) in Doucet, P. and Laurin, C. (eds.) *Problems of Psychosis: International Colloquium Series, 1969*. Amsterdam: Excerpt Medica.

20 Rosenfeld, H. (1972) A critical appreciation of James Strachey's paper on the nature of the therapeutic action of psychoanalysis. *International Journal of Psychoanalysis* 5: 455–461.

21 Rosenfeld, H. (1973) Negative therapeutic reaction. In Giovachini, P. (ed.) *Tactics and Techniques in Psychoanalytic Therapy, Vol II*: 217–228. New York: Jason Aronson.

22 Rosenfeld, H. (1974) A discussion of the paper by Ralph R. Greenson on 'Transference: Freud or Klein'. *International Journal of Psychoanalysis* 55: 49–51.

23 Rosenfeld, H. (1978a) Some therapeutic factors in psychoanalysis. *International Journal of Psychoanalytic Psychotherapy* 7: 152–164.

24 Rosenfeld, H. (1978b) Notes on the psychopathology and psychoanalytic treatment of some borderline patients. *International Journal of Psychoanalysis* 59: 215–221.

25 Rosenfeld, H. (1979) Difficulties in the psychoanalytic treatment of borderline patients. In Le Boit, J. and Capponi, A. (eds.) *Advances in the Psychotherapy of the Borderline Patient*: 187–206. New York: Jason Aronson.

26 Rosenfeld, H. (1981) On the psychopathology and treatment of psychotic patients (Historical and comparative reflections). In Grotstein, J. S. (ed.) *Do I Dare Disturb the Universe?*: 167–180. Beverley Hills: Caesura Press.

27 Rosenfeld, H. (1983) Primitive object relations and mechanisms. *International Journal of Psychoanalysis* 64: 261–267.

28 Rosenfeld, H. (1987) *Impasse and Interpretation: Therapeutic and Anti-Therapeutic Factors in the Psychoanalytic Treatment of Psychotic, Borderline, and Neurotic Patients.* London: Routledge.

29 Rosenfeld, H. (1988) On masochism: A theoretical and clinical approach. In Click, R. A. and Meyers, D. I. (eds.) *Masochism: Current Psychoanalytic Perspectives*: 151–174. Hillsdale, NJ: The Analytic Press.

30 Rosenfeld, H. (2001) *Herbert Rosenfeld at Work: The Italian Seminars* (edited by F. de Masi). London: Karnac.

References

Bálint, A. and Bálint, M. (1939) On transference and counter-transference. *International Journal of Psycho-Analysis* 20: 223–230.

Bion, W. R. (1959) Attacks on linking. *International Journal of Psychoanalysis* 40: 308–315. Reprinted in Bion, W.R. (1967) *Second Thoughts*. London: Heinemann: pp. 138–152. In *The Complete Works of W.R. Bion 4*. London: Karnac: pp. 247–265.

Bion, W. R. (1967) Notes on memory and desire. *Psychoanalytic Forum* 2: 271–280. Reprinted in Bott Spillius E., ed. (1988). *Melanie Klein Today, Vol. 2: Mainly practice*. London: Routledge: pp. 17–21.

Brandchaft, B. (1986) British object relations theory and self psychology. *Progress in Self-Psychology* 2: 245–272.

de Masi, F. (2001) Introduction to *Herbert Rosenfeld at Work*. London: Karnac.

Freud, S. (1911a) *Psycho-Analytic Notes on an Autobiographical Account of a Case of Paranoia (Dementia Paranoides). Standard Edition of the Complete Psychological works of Sigmund Freud, Volume* 12: 3–82. London: Hogarth.

Freud, S. (1911b) Formulations on the two principles of mental functioning. In *The Standard Edition of the Complete Psychological Works of Sigmund Freud, Volume XII*: 213–226. London: Hogarth.

Freud, S. (1912) Recommendations to physicians practising psychoanalysis. In *The Standard Edition of the Complete Psychological Works of Sigmund Freud, Volume XII*: 109–120. London: Hogarth.

Freud, S. (1914) On narcissism: An introduction. In *The Standard Edition of the Complete Psychological Works of Sigmund Freud, Volume 14*. London: Hogarth.

Freud, S. (1921) Group psychology and the analysis of the ego. In *Standard Edition of the Complete Psychological works of Sigmund Freud, Volume 18*: 67–143. London: Hogarth.

Freud, S. (1925) Negation. In *The Standard Edition of the Complete Psychological Works of Sigmund Freud, Volume XIX*: 233–240. London: Hogarth.

Gitelson, M. (1958) On ego distortion. *International Journal of Psychoanalysis* 39: 245–256.

Greenson, R. R. (1974) Transference: Freud or Klein. *International Journal of Psychoanalysis* 55: 37–48.

Grosskurth, P. (1986) *Melanie Klein: Her World and her Work*. London: Hodder and Stoughton.

Grotstein, J. (1982) *Splitting and Projective Identification*. New York: Jason Aronson.

Heimann, Paula (1950) On counter-transference. *International Journal of Psycho-Analysis* 31: 81–84. Republished in Paula Heimann (1989) *About Children and Children-No-Longer*. London: Routledge: pp. 73–79.

Hinshelwood, R.D. (2006) Early repression mechanism: Social, conceptual and personal factors in the historical development of certain psychoanalytic ideas arising from reflection upon Melanie Klein's unpublished (1934) notes prior to her paper on the depressive position. *Psychoanalysis and History* 8: 5–42.

Hinshelwood, R. D. (2008) Melanie Klein and countertransference: A note on some archival material. *Psychoanalysis and History* 10: 95–113.

Jacobson, E. (1954) The self and the object world. *The Psychoanalytic Study of the Child* 9: 75–127.

King, P. and Steiner, R. (1991) *The Freud-Klein Controversies 1941–1945*. London: Routledge.

Klein, M. (1930) The importance of symbol-formation in the development of the ego. In *The Writings of Melanie Klein, Volume 1*: 219–232. London: Hogarth.

Klein, M. (1932) *The Psycho-Analysis of Children*. London: Hogarth. Republished (1975) as *The Writings of Melanie Klein, Volume 2*. London: Hogarth.

Klein, M. (1946) Notes on some schizoid mechanisms. *International Journal of Psycho-Analysis* 27: 99–110; republished (1952) in Melanie Klein, Paula Heimann, Susan Isaacs and Joan Riviere, *Developments in Psycho-Analysis*: 292–320. London: Hogarth. Republished in *The Writings of Melanie Klein, Volume 3*: 1–24. London: Hogarth.

Klein, M. (1957) *Envy and Gratitude*. London: Hogarth. Republished (1975) in *The Writings of Melanie Klein, Volume 2*: 176–235. London: Hogarth.

Klein, K. (1959) Autobiography. Wellcome Library Archives, PP/RMK/E.6/3, p. 24. And retrieved June 2022: https://melanie-klein-trust.org.uk/wp-content/uploads/2019/06/MK_full_autobiography.pdf

Klein, M. (2017) *Lectures on Technique* (edited by J. Steiner). London: Routledge.

Mahler, M. S. (1952) On child psychosis and schizophrenia – Autistic and symbiotic infantile psychoses. *Psychoanalytic Study of the Child* 7: 286–305.

Ogden, T. H. (1994) The concept of interpretive action. *Psychoanalytic Quarterly* 63: 219–245.

O'Shaughnessy, E. (1988) Herbert Rosenfeld: Impasse and interpretation. *Journal of Child Psychotherapy* 14: 99–101.

Rosenfeld, A. (2016) My father, Herbert Rosenfeld. *International Forum of Psychoanalysis* 25: 220–228.

Segal, H. (1957) Notes on symbol formation. *International Journal of Psychoanalysis* 38: 391–397.

Segal, H. (1978) On symbolism. *International Journal of Psychoanalysis* 59: 315–319.

Segal, H. (2008) Discussion of Ron Britton's Paper. In J. Steiner (ed.) *Rosenfeld in Retrospect*. London: Routledge.

Steiner, J. (2008) *Rosenfeld in Retrospect*. London: Retrospect.

Steiner, R. (2001) Foreword to *Herbert Rosenfeld at Work* (edited by Franco de Masi): ix–xiv. London: Karnac.

Stolorow, R. D. and Atwood, G. E. (1984) Psychoanalytic phenomenology: Toward a science of human experience. *Psychoanalytic Inquiry* 4: 87–105.

Stolorow, R. D., Atwood, G. E. and Ross, J. M. (1978) The representational world in psychoanalytic therapy. *International Review of Psychoanalysis* 5: 247–256.

Strachey, J. (1934) The nature of the therapeutic action of psychoanalysis. *International Journal of Psycho-Analysis* 15: 127–159. Republished (1969) *International Journal of Psycho-Analysis* 50: 275–192.

Index

Printed in the United States
by Baker & Taylor Publisher Services